HANDMADE
IN MELBOURNE

'Handmade' is a wonderfully descriptive term.
It evokes a sense of total creativity, the capacity to turn common
ingredients or materials into something of purpose, and often of
great beauty. It's a rare skill to be able to achieve both.
This book celebrates that skill, and the passion, commitment and
values of those who have made handmade their life's work.
I hope its publication will encourage more and more of us not only
to attempt to be creative to whatever standard we are capable,
but also to celebrate those who do what they do, by hand.

Geoff Slattery

Geoff Slattery Publishing Pty Ltd

140 Harbour Esplanade, Docklands, Victoria 3008

www.geoffslattery.com.au

National Library of Australia

Cataloguing-in-Publication

Phyland, Jan.

      Handmade in Melbourne.

      ISBN 9780975796498.

      1. Handicraft - Victoria - Melbourne. 2. Artisans - Victoria - Melbourne. 3. Small business - Victoria - Melbourne. I. De Silva, Janet. II. Cambray, Dean, 1965- . III. Title.

      680.099451

Publisher: Stephanie Wood

Designer: Oliver Newbery

Editor: Roslyn Grundy

Researchers: Catherine Mills and Janelle Ward

Photo Manager: Sally Prideaux

Produced in China through Bookbuilders

HANDMADE

IN MELBOURNE

JAN PHYLAND & JANET DE SILVA

BEAUTIFUL THINGS
FROM 80 CREATIVE PEOPLE

PHOTOGRAPHY DEAN CAMBRAY

gspbooks

CONTENTS

FOREWORD
BY ADAM ELLIOT 8

INTRODUCTION
BY JAN PHYLAND AND
JANET DE SILVA 10

ATTIRE 14

JOHANNA PRESTON & PETR ZLY
{ SHOEMAKERS } 16

VICTORIA HASLAM
{ KNITWEAR DESIGNER } 18

CHARLES MAIMONE
{ TAILOR } 20

PAUL ANTHONY
{ FASHION DESIGNER } 22

GWENDOLYNNE BURKIN
{ FASHION DESIGNER } 24

NATALIE BEGG
{ LINGERIE / FASHION DESIGNER } 26

SARTI TAILORS
{ TAILORS } 28

NIKKI GABRIEL
{ KNITWEAR AND TEXTILE DESIGNER } 30

BRENDAN DWYER
{ SHOEMAKER } 32

EUGENE NOTERMANS
{ SHIRTMAKER / TAILOR } 34

STEWART RUSSELL
{ TEXTILE PRINTER / ARTIST } 36

GEORGIA CHAPMAN
{ FASHION DESIGNER } 38

ADORNMENT 40

MASAKO SHIBATA
{ TEXTILE ARTIST } 42

JULIE FLEMING
{ MILLINER } 44

MARY ODORCIC
{ JEWELLER } 46

KATE BOULTON
{ BUTTON MAKER } 48

FIORINA GOLOTTA
{ JEWELLER } 50

BRENDAN O'KEEFE
{ EYEWEAR DESIGNER } 52

KATE TUCKER
{ TEXTILE / HANDBAG MAKER } 54

MELISSA JACKSON
{ MILLINER } 56

LYNLEY TRAEGER
{ JEWELLER / WALKING STICK MAKER } 58

JULIA DEVILLE
{ JEWELLER / TAXIDERMIST } 60

ADRIAN LEWIS
{ JEWELLER } 62

MOYA DELANY
{ FASHION ACCESSORIES DESIGNER } 64

CAMILLA GOUGH
{ JEWELLER } 66

RICHARD NYLON
{ MILLINER } 68

MARCOS DAVIDSON
{ JEWELLER } 70

MATT THOMSON
{ BAG MAKER } 72

ILKA WHITE
{ WEAVER AND TEXTILE DESIGNER } 74

HOMEWARES 76

JULIE CAINES
{ TASSEL MAKER } 78

MAUREEN WILLIAMS
{ GLASS ARTIST } 80

ANTON GERNER
{ FURNITURE MAKER } 82

CATHY HOPE
{ QUILTER } 84

JEREMY WILKINS & STEPHEN KENT
{ FURNITURE MAKERS } 86

KYLE DE KUIJER
& STEPHANIE FLEMMING
{ HOMEWARES DESIGNERS } 88

MARK SHEIL
{ METAL ARTISAN } 90

GEOFFREY MANCE
{ LIGHTING DESIGNER } 92

WILLIAM MATTHYSEN
{ CLOCK MAKER } 94

FRED GANIM
{ TILE PAINTER } 96

CAMERON COMER
{ HOME ACCESSORIES DESIGNER / STYLIST } 98

BARBARA RICHARDS
{ LAMPSHADE MAKER } 100

CHRIS PLUMRIDGE
{ CERAMICIST } 102

WENDY GOLDEN
{ BASKET MAKER } 104

MARC PASCAL
{ LIGHTING AND CERAMICS DESIGNER } 106

PETER MCLISKY
{ STONE CARVER } 108

GREG HATTON
{ FURNITURE MAKER } 110

SIMON LLOYD
{ PRODUCT DESIGNER } 112

ANNA LORENZETTO
{ LEATHER HOMEWARES DESIGNER } 114

VICKI MURFETT
{ SHELL ARTIST } 116

KRIS COAD
{ CERAMICIST } 118

MARK MARINATO
{ MIRROR MAKER } 120

ANNA CHARLESWORTH
{ METAL ARTIST } 122

BERN EMMERICHS
{ CERAMICIST } 124

ANDREW WOOD
{ WOOD WORKER } 126

PHILIP STOKES
{ GLASS ARTIST } 128

PLEASURE 130

JAMES CATTELL
{ TOY MAKER / SCULPTOR } 132

MARIANNA DI BARTOLO
{ BISCUIT AND SWEET MAKER } 134

BECK WHEELER
{ ARTIST / TEXTILE SCULPTOR } 136

JACK POMPEI
{ BOAT BUILDER } 138

BENEDICT PUGLISI
{ STRINGED INSTRUMENT MAKER } 140

NEIL OKE
{ SURFBOARD MAKER } 142

JUDY CAMERON
{ TOY MAKER } 144

LACHLAN FISHER
{ CRICKET BAT MAKER } 146

ADRIENNE CHISHOLM
{ PUPPET MAKER / DESIGNER } 148

IAN WATCHORN
{ STRINGED INSTRUMENT MAKER } 150

ALANA WATERSON & SARA DICKINS
{ STATIONERY DESIGNERS } 152

LEON PETROFF
{ VIOLIN MAKER } 154

DANIEL CHIRICO
{ BAKER } 156

GRACIA HABY & LOUISE JENNISON
{ JOURNAL MAKERS / ARTISTS } 158

CAROLYN IMLACH
{ SOAP MAKER } 160

ARNO BACKES
{ CHOCOLATIER } 162

JACK SPIRA
{ GUITAR MAKER } 164

JANE WIFFEN
{ CUPCAKE MAKER } 166

ANITA MIKEDIS
{ BOTANICAL HOMEWARES DESIGNER } 168

JOANNE SCHOOF
{ CANDLE MAKER } 170

PETER LANCASTER
{ LITHOGRAPHER } 172

DAVID COLES
{ PAINT MAKER } 174

EMMA COWAN
{ CARD DESIGNER / ARTIST } 176

IRWIN AND MCLAREN BOOKBINDERS
{ BOOKBINDERS } 178

JOANNE SAUNDERS
{ RECORDER MAKER } 180

DIRECTORY 182

FOREWORD
{ ADAM ELLIOT }

Why is Melbourne the handmade hub of Australia? Why is it home to so many creative souls? Is it because our community is more encouraging of their work? Are there more creative educational institutions? Are there economic factors such as a lower cost of living compared with, say, Sydney, that allow people to be struggling artisans?

These might all be factors, but my view is that the weather is the key. I love how Melbourne's winter, like a fat man on a park bench, pushes the other seasons out of the way. The city's climate is so much more conducive to creativity. If we had the weather of Queensland, I'm sure we wouldn't be half as productive. In fact, recently I went to a motivational conference for artists in Surfers Paradise for which hundreds signed up, but very few fronted. It was a beautiful day and I'm sure they were all down at the beach.

I am one of Melbourne's creative souls and have always considered my work handmade. My claymated films are entirely created by hand; there is not one single frame of computer-generated imagery. I like this fact and so do audiences. They love seeing the fingerprints on my characters; it reminds them that what they are seeing is real, tactile and tangible.

This is something I realised and appreciated long before I went to film school. For five years I sold hand-painted T-shirts at the St Kilda Esplanade Arts and Craft Market, which is now more than 36 years old. Every Sunday, I'd sit trying to sell my individually hand-painted 'Murray the Tap-Dancing Dim Sim' garments. I put them in brown pizza boxes with the lid cut out so you could see the design. They were very popular; not so much because they were funny, but rather because they were handmade by me, a strange little bald man sitting in the rain.

Whatever the reason Melbourne spawns and attracts such creativity, the people you are about to meet in the following glossy pages are but a few of the many who lurk and work quietly in their studios and sheds. In content worlds of their own, the hours drift by as they draw, buzz, drill, sand, paint and shape, fully focused on creating. We artisans are indeed lucky souls, for we have jobs that we are passionate about. I itch to get into my studio each morning and find it hard to leave in the evening. Sometimes I am so engrossed in my work that I forget to eat, go the bathroom or ring my mother for her birthday.

Read on and engage with Melbourne's fecund array of clever artists, artisans and craftspeople who wiggle their creative digits to produce beautiful, functional and unique pieces. Who knows, they may inspire you to dump the internet and venture down into your own back shed to create something gloriously handmade. ✻

Melbourne-based Adam Elliot was the creator and director of Harvie Krumpet, *which won an Academy Award in 2003 for Best Animated Short Film.*

INTRODUCTION

{ JAN PHYLAND AND JANET DE SILVA }

In a world where everything from furniture to fashion is cloned and mass-produced, the handmade item stands apart. In the finely stitched seam of a bespoke suit, in the subtle fingerprints left on a rolled ball of soap or in the intricate detail in a deftly worked piece of jewellery, there is integrity. Less tangibly, the handmade item carries the personal signature of its creator and a sense of time; the time spent polishing or stitching, carving, shaping or moulding.

Whether valued for its sophistication, its pureness of form or for its simplicity, a handmade item has been made with care. Even if produced in small batches, as are cast ceramic vessels or screen-printed fabrics, handmade items have an air of individuality – if only through a slight alteration in form or a tiny imperfection – to be celebrated rather than scorned.

Over the past few years there has been a global resurgence of interest in handmade products of quality, substance and personality. At a domestic level, knitting and crafts such as quilting and toy-making are booming, fuelled by a vibrant online craft community and groups such as Stitch n' Bitch. International trend forecaster Faith Popcorn expresses the prevailing mood eloquently: "Smooth, shiny and uniform is now equated to crude and cheap, especially when compared to the individuality of hand-crafted products. We are very hungry for things that have touched human hands. Handmade things with all their wonderful imperfections have a very rare value."

In Melbourne, a city that has a rich history of fostering creativity, stores such as Counter at Craft Victoria, Wilkins and Kent, and Alice Euphemia are glorious shrines to handmade items. Over the past few years, markets dedicated to emerging artists, designers and craftspeople have sprung up, including the Rose Street Artists Market in Fitzroy and the ReadyMadeMarket, run by the National Design Centre at Federation Square.

LIVES OF FULFILMENT

There was a similar shift in the 19th century during the Arts and Crafts Movement, which sought to counter the perceived dehumanising effects of industrialisation with work of authenticity and meaning. One of the movement's principal founders, Englishman William Morris, championed handcrafted items, claiming they represented "the expression by man of his joy in labour". Real art, Morris said, must be made by the people for the people to bring happiness to both maker and user.

Indeed, as we discovered while visiting the Melbourne artists, artisans and craftspeople profiled in this book, their work brings them immeasurable fulfilment. They are a passionate breed for whom work is more a calling than a career; many knew from an early age that they wanted to be ceramicists, jewellers or designers. Joanne Saunders *(see page 180)*, for example, knew at 15 that she wanted to make recorders for a living. Most of those profiled speak of a deep need to express themselves through their craft. They have an almost superhuman drive to create, frequently working around the clock to meet a deadline or complete an order. Solitary nights spent hunched over sewing machines and long weekends at workbenches are common. The subjects in *Handmade in Melbourne* frequently mention the pleasure they get from the physical, rhythmic or meditative process of creating – knitting, weaving, hammering, chiselling or carving – and of being oblivious to the passing of time. After 20 years carving cricket bats, for example, Lachlan Fisher still finds it the most enjoyable thing he does *(see page 146)*. "Carving the first bat of the day, I develop sweat, rhythm and perseverance. It's immensely satisfying." Toy maker Judy Cameron *(see page 144)* often finds herself toiling until the early hours of the morning. "I lose myself quite easily in the work. I get such pleasure from seeing something that starts as a flat piece of fabric transformed into a wonderful little character."

Many struggle to earn a living from their craft and second jobs are not uncommon. Indeed, some confess to being too nervous to tally the hours they spend toiling for fear of discovering the real cost of their chosen craft. For them, financial success is rarely a driving factor: gratification comes from taking an idea or design and turning it into something to be admired, cherished or handed down through the generations.

A CRAFT OF GENERATIONS

For some *Handmade* subjects, their craft has itself been passed down through generations. Boatbuilder Jack Pompei *(see page 138)*, for example, comes from a family of boatbuilders whose business dates back to the early 1900s. Others inherited an interest in craft, or had creative parents and grandparents. Textile artist Masako Shibata's mother was an artisan and kimono historian *(see page 42)*. Instrument maker Ian Watchorn's *(see page 150)* parents were piano teachers and choirmasters.

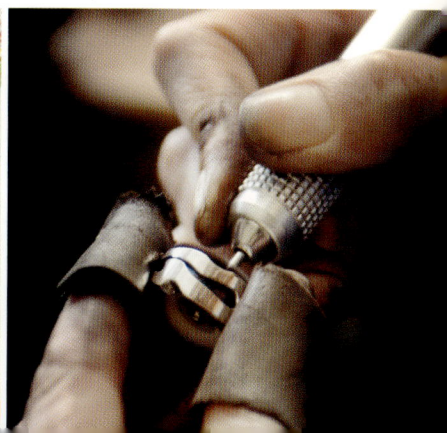

There are those who came to their craft after a life-changing event such as a car accident, mid-life crisis, job retrenchment or a desire to call their own tune. Ceramicist Chris Plumridge *(see page 102)* threw himself into ceramics with a sense of urgency after being diagnosed with a potentially life-threatening illness. Some *Handmade* subjects are largely self-taught. Jack Spira *(see page 164)* taught himself to make guitars, initially selling them at folk festivals and refining his skills over time. Others trained under accomplished migrant artisans who settled in Melbourne after World War II. Jeweller Marcos Davidson *(see page 70)* and tailor Charles Maimone *(see page 20)* both recall a time when Melbourne's lanes and arcades were awash with strange accents and workshops full of European craftsmen.

The accents may have softened but the city's lanes and arcades are still home to artisans, craftspeople and designers, some working in solitude, some sharing studios, and others finding a community in places such as the Nicholas Building, with its labyrinth of corridors leading to more than 100 tenants, including jewellers and milliners, cobblers and button makers. A hop, skip and a few lattes away in Elizabeth Street, the Art Deco Carlow House similarly boasts a cluster of jewellers and designers. Promising newer hubs of creative activity include the reincarnated Abbotsford Convent, home to an increasing number of artisans' workshops, including that of glass artist Philip Stokes *(see page 128)*. The sprawling complex of buildings, serenely located on the banks of the Yarra River, has been preserved as an arts, education and culture precinct. And in the west, suburbs such as Footscray, Brooklyn and Seddon are thriving as artisans move in to take advantage of cheaper rents and larger spaces. Others work from historic inner-city warehouses, in sheds set amid neglected greenery in outer-suburban backyards, or in home kitchens and lounge rooms.

Regardless of their location, visiting the *Handmade* subjects' workspaces was often as inspirational as the artisans themselves. What many lacked in comforts such as heating they made up for with an energy-charged atmosphere. Invariably, the spaces were cluttered with the raw materials of their trade, from piles of metal, stone and wood, to buttons, beads, fabric and feathers; high-tech equipment or tools that have not changed in centuries; and the treasures and detritus from a life spent gathering and collecting. Indeed, many of the artisans have scavenger tendencies, haunting auction rooms, junk shops and charity shops, their wares based on recycled materials. Toy maker and sculptor James Cattell scours scrap metal yards *(see page 132)* and accessories maker Moya Delany gathers feathers *(see page 64)*. Often this hunter-gatherer instinct is driven by a keen sense of responsibility to society and the environment. Greg Hatton *(see page 110)*, for example, raids river banks to collect willow, a noxious pest, from which he crafts his furniture.

A CELEBRATION OF DIVERSITY

Choosing the subjects to profile in *Handmade in Melbourne* was an enormously challenging task – we could have produced many more volumes. Within the limitations of space and time, however, we wanted to celebrate the diversity of handmade goods being produced in Melbourne. In these pages, then, we've brought together 80 disparate talents, from knitters, bakers and candle makers to internationally known glass blowers, ceramicists and jewellers. In an attempt to broaden the book still further, we asked each subject to offer one or more source of inspiration. The result of this request is a fascinating insider's view of Melbourne – the craftspeople our subjects most admire; their favourite suppliers of raw materials; little-known markets, secondhand shops, bookshops, galleries and websites; sculptures and places of natural beauty. You'll find a directory of our subjects and their inspirations in the back of the book.

Creating *Handmade in Melbourne* has been an amazing journey through a world we feel privileged to have glimpsed. It has given us a new appreciation of the value of handmade items, in spiritual, emotional and monetary terms. Some people may find it difficult to justify the cost of a handmade candle or ball of soap, let alone a tailored suit or beautifully hand-crafted dining table. But to understand the expense of some handmade products is to understand the preciousness of time. It is to understand the value of individuality, and the durable, enduring nature of the products in these pages. All of them fit the William Morris ideal of bringing joy to both maker and user. ✾

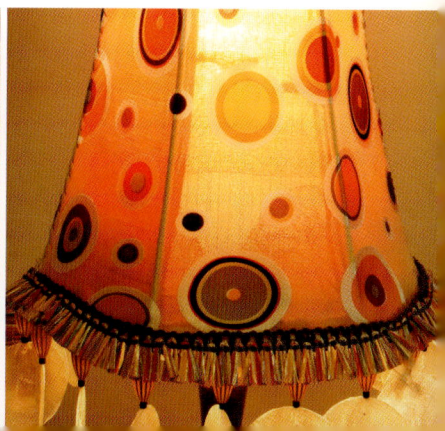

ATTIRE

FASHION
TAILORING
KNITWEAR AND TEXTILE DESIGN
SHOES

JOHANNA PRESTON
& PETR ZLY
{ SHOEMAKERS }

VICTORIA HASLAM
{ KNITWEAR DESIGNER }

CHARLES MAIMONE
{ TAILOR }

PAUL ANTHONY
{ FASHION DESIGNER }

GWENDOLYNNE BURKIN
{ FASHION DESIGNER }

NATALIE BEGG
{ LINGERIE / FASHION DESIGNER }

SARTI TAILORS
{ TAILORS }

NIKKI GABRIEL
{ KNITWEAR AND TEXTILE DESIGNER }

BRENDAN DWYER
{ SHOEMAKER }

EUGENE NOTERMANS
{ SHIRTMAKER / TAILOR }

STEWART RUSSELL
{ TEXTILE PRINTER / ARTIST }

GEORGIA CHAPMAN
{ FASHION DESIGNER }

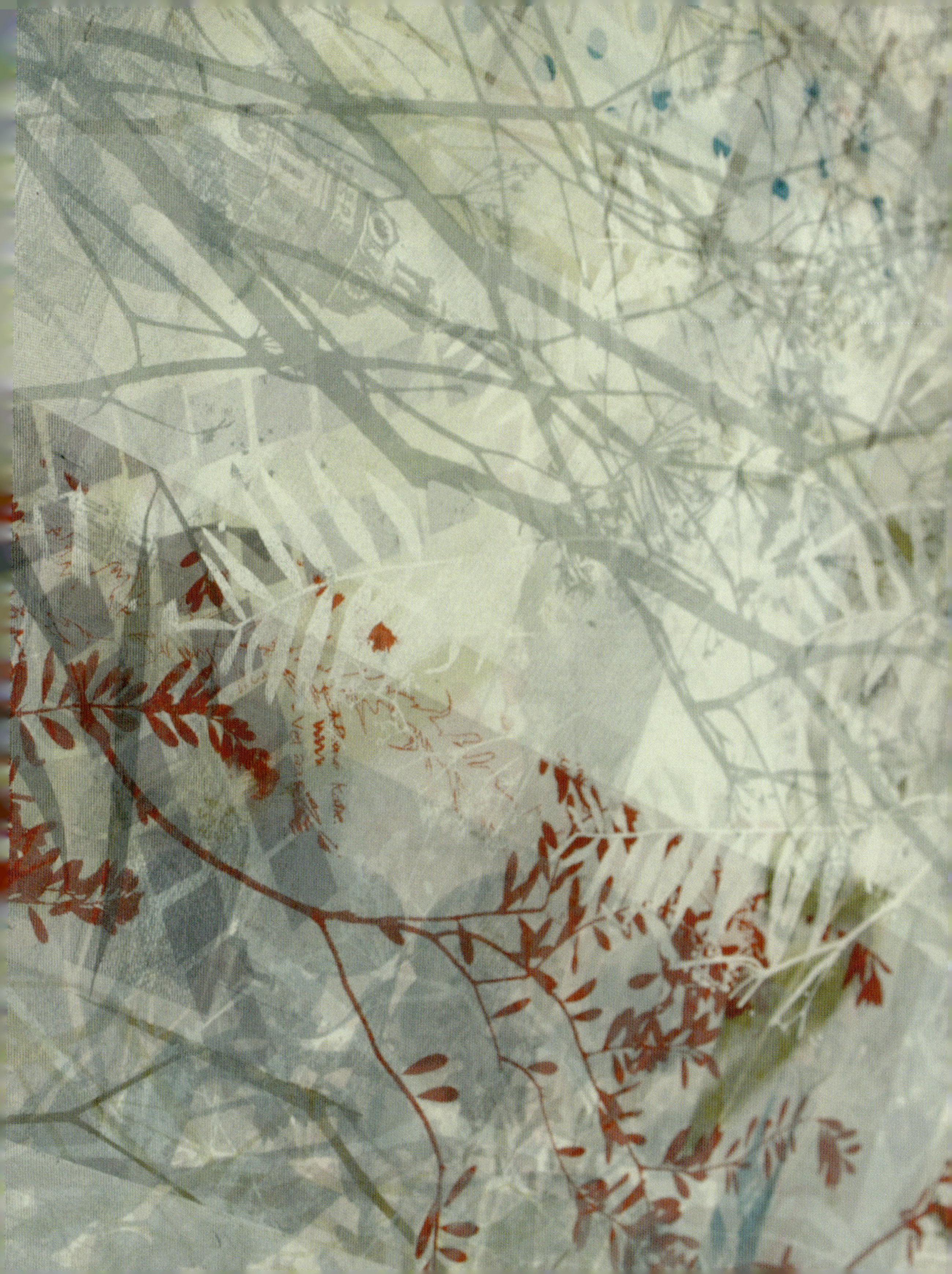

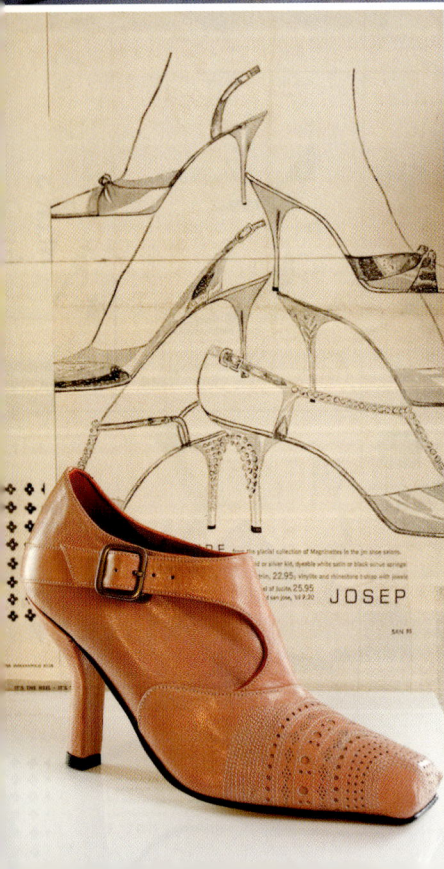

JOHANNA PRESTON & PETR ZLY

{ SHOEMAKERS }

Johanna Preston has a confession: she is completely obsessed with shoes. Her footwear fetish began in childhood, fuelled by relatives who brought her exotic shoes back from overseas trips – moccasins hand-beaded by Native Americans, glass-beaded golden slippers from Asia, and slim, chocolate leather wedges from Italy. That fetish has blossomed into a thriving business that counts Australian actors Sigrid Thornton and Toni Collette among its fans.

It was Johanna's husband, sculptor Petr Zly, who suggested they pool their talents and turn her passion into a career. Gaining a certificate in orthopaedic and bespoke footwear and completing three intensive courses with a Bulgarian master shoemaker in Adelaide, Johanna established the business with Petr in 1994. It was an immediate hit, combining Petr's sculptural eye with Johanna's craftsmanship to create funky, unconventional designs with individual styling.

Behind their showroom, wallpapered with vintage shoe advertisements, lies a labyrinth of dusty rooms cluttered with bolts of leather, boxes of wooden shoe lasts, traditional hand tools and machinery. It is here that Johanna and Petr meticulously craft up to 20 pairs of shoes a week, inspired by everything from the soft ballet-like slippers of a Jane Austen heroine to traditional Mary Janes, which in their hands become sexy and grown-up.

Depending on the style, each shoe might undergo up to 150 processes and take anywhere between seven and 50 hours to complete. "Ideas come to me when I'm doing mundane things – it's rare for us to go looking for inspiration," says Johanna. "Some of my best ideas come when I'm driving my son home from his violin lesson." *(Preston Zly Design, rear 219 Smith Street, Fitzroy. Full details, page 189.)*

INSPIRATIONS

{ INDUSTRIA } "For its strange and eclectic collection of crockery and furniture from hospitals, asylums and other places." *(202 Gertrude Street, Fitzroy.)*

{ COLLINGWOOD CHILDREN'S FARM } "To be able to step back into a rural setting in the middle of the industrial inner city of Melbourne and be reminded of times past." *(St Heliers Street, Abbotsford.)*

{ SONSA FOODS } "For the lovely Turkish family that runs this establishment, stocking it with an amazing array of international produce such as dried white mulberries, dried capsicum paste and the cheapest preserved lemons." *(152 Smith Street, Collingwood.)*

OPPOSITE: *The unconventional creations of shoe-obsessed Johanna Preston and her husband, sculptor Petr Zly, have a passionate following.*

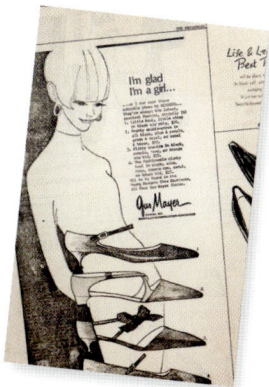

VICTORIA HASLAM
{ KNITWEAR DESIGNER }

From a distance, it's not hard to imagine a warrior from China's historic terracotta army wearing one of Victoria Haslam's woollen hats. But up close, they are anything but warlike. Eye-catching colours and whimsical embellishments give Victoria's headgear an offbeat feel.

Knitting has always been part of Victoria's life. Growing up in Philadelphia, her mother taught her to knit, crochet, embroider and sew. While studying art in the United States and later Rome, she often knitted her own scarves and clothes. And when her two sons were born, naturally she knitted them a collection of natty jumpers and matching hats.

When she moved to Melbourne in 2001 and was constantly stopped by people asking where they could buy the knits her children wore, Victoria realised she could turn hobby into business.

Today, she uses locally sourced wools to create a collection of knitted hats, scarves and wraps for children and adults under the Pygmalion Handknits label. Rejecting the traditional beanie style, Victoria wanted her hats to feature bold, silhouette-changing constructions. Up to five finely knitted panels are crocheted together to give strength to the helmet-like form, and a seam on to which she can add details such as beading or embroidery. Their geometric patterns are inspired by Turkish socks and Persian rugs, their architectural shapes by Thai temples, and their rich colours used by Peru's Inca civilisation.

A simple box-top, three-panelled hat takes up to 12 hours to complete, while the more detailed five-panel Gum Nut style take 24 hours. Pygmalion hats range in price from $50 to $120, while wraps and scarves are priced from $50.

"There is a real palpability of time in these hats – time used in design, construction and in finishing," Victoria says. *(Contact and stockist details, page 185.)* 🐾

INSPIRATIONS

{ WONDOFLEX YARN CRAFT CENTRE } "A hangar-like space crammed with most of knitters' desires." *(1353 Malvern Road, Malvern.)*

{ THE BUTTON SHOP } "Quaint, with retro charm. The diverse and sometimes rare notions are offered in a genteel and professional manner."
(181 Glenferrie Road, Malvern.)

{ EST AUSTRALIA } "The hand-crafted soaps and lotions in this deliciously perfumed store are to-die-for." *(134 Auburn Road, Hawthorn East; see also page 160.)*

OPPOSITE: *Rich colours and unusual sillhouettes characterise Victoria Haslam's handknits.*

CHARLES MAIMONE

{ TAILOR }

For almost four decades, Charles Maimone has measured and fitted some of the country's most powerful businessmen and politicians in his nondescript two-room studio. Each has become the proud owner of one of the tailor's beautifully crafted suits. Time seems to have stood still in Charles's workspace: his tiny front salon holds little more than a small rack of suits and an old red velvet winged chair; in the workshop behind are a couple of worn workbenches and a 100-year-old Singer sewing machine. Even his assistant has been part of the landscape for three decades.

Aged 14, Charles followed in his brother's footsteps to become an apprentice to a master tailor in Sicily. When his brother migrated to Melbourne, Charles followed soon after and the two worked together as tailors. In 1967, Charles went out on his own, moving to a city location and quickly establishing a select clientele: politicians from nearby Spring Street, high-flying businessmen stopping by for fittings on their way to lunch at fine restaurants such as the Florentino or the Society, and international guests staying at Melbourne's then most fashionable hotel, the Southern Cross. Many have remained loyal to Charles since those early days – one gentleman even has his suits sent to America, where he now lives.

With so much experience, Charles says he can tell by looking at a client which style and cut will suit him best. These days, he rarely works with a pattern, preferring to cut directly from measurements. Each suit, made with the finest fabrics from London, Brussels, Paris or Milan, takes up to four weeks to complete and costs between $2500 and $3500.

Charles likens having a bespoke suit made to having a portrait painted: the result is painstakingly crafted and customised with just one person in mind. "If you add heart to something done with your hands and mind, it will always be your best."
(Charles Maimone, 1 Crossley Street, Melbourne. Full details, page 187.) 🪡

INSPIRATIONS

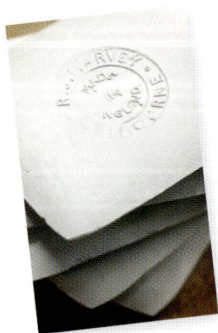

{ R J HARVEY & CO } "I have been buying all my tailoring trims, like zips and buttons, from here for 45 years." *(Level 3, 37 Swanston Street, Melbourne.)*

{ DORMEUIL } "Great fabrics – I have used them for 45 years." *(Level 10, 22 William Street, Melbourne.)*

{ PELLEGRINI'S ESPRESSO BAR } "For 39 years, I have averaged about two cappuccinos from here every day!" *(66 Bourke Street, Melbourne.)*

OPPOSITE (CLOCKWISE FROM TOP): *Suits waiting for finishing touches; assistant tailor Flavio Mallamaci; and Charles Maimone.*

PAUL ANTHONY

{ FASHION DESIGNER }

Asked if he always wanted to be a fashion designer, Paul Anthony whips out a photograph. The faded black-and-white snap shows a three-year-old Paul wearing a simple sleeveless dress that belonged to his mother. It did not take Paul long to channel his love of dressing up in a new direction: by seven, he was running up clothes for his sisters' Barbie dolls on a machine he badgered his mother into giving him.

Today, Paul uses traditional tailoring methods to create classic one-off pieces using vintage and contemporary fabrics. His clients are mostly older women with an appreciation of design who want pieces that reflect their personality. A self-described perfectionist, Paul eschews "instant fashion fixes" and says his work is the antithesis of minimalism. It is informed by an innate sense of proportion and style and his admiration for the meticulously tailored designs of the late Oleg Cassini, who dressed the American First Lady Jacqueline Kennedy in the 1960s.

In 1998, while studying fashion in Melbourne, Paul won a scholarship to study at England's Ravensbourne College of Design and Communication, then spent six months in the studio of influential British designer Vivienne Westwood before returning to Melbourne. He tried working for other fashion houses, hated it, and finally established his own design company in 2000. That year, he took out the Mercedes Young Designer Award at Melbourne's Spring Fashion Week.

For all his immersion in city life, Paul's rural upbringing in the Riverina District of New South Wales continues to influence his work, particularly when choosing fabric colours. "I never thought the country offered me anything," he says. "But I now look back and see how beautiful it was, particularly the landscapes and colours." *(Paul Anthony Designs, 81a Chapel Street, Windsor. Full details, page 182.)* 🌸

INSPIRATIONS

{ THE DANCING QUEEN } "They have wonderful vintage fabrics." *(327 Lennox Street, Richmond.)*

{ EUROTRASH } "Great recycled clothing, particularly from European designers." *(228 Chapel Street, Prahran.)*

{ LINDA BLACK RECYCLED FASHION } "The furriers at Linda Black deal in amazing old fur coats." *(151 Chapel Street, Windsor.)*

OPPOSITE: *Paul Anthony, a self-described "maximalist", in his studio.*

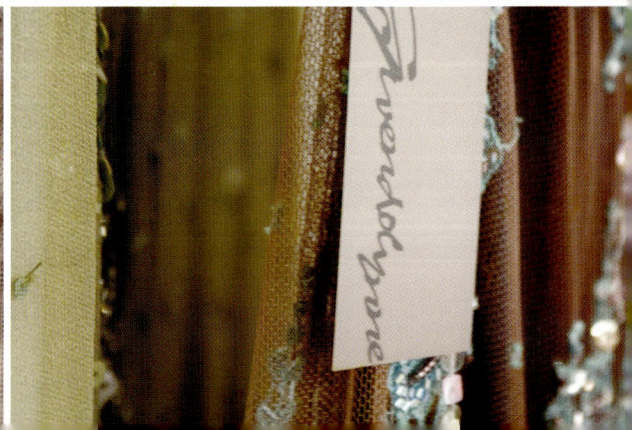

GWENDOLYNNE BURKIN
{ FASHION DESIGNER }

Pinned to a board in Gwendolynne Burkin's studio is a postcard of a woman with alabaster skin stretching languidly on a bed, draped in a white sheet. *Phaedra*, painted by French artist Alexandre Cabanel in 1880, is a muse for the designer and an image she hopes to evoke in a forthcoming photo shoot. It also hints at Gwendolynne's style: historical references intertwined with contemporary fashion silhouettes.

Sitting at a large workbench in the atelier above her shop, Gwendolynne is busily perfecting a jacket lining, surrounded by accoutrements that reveal her twin passions – fashion history and fabric. Bolts of intricately beaded fabric are propped in a corner ready to be cut, and racks are hung with brown paper patterns and garments that pay homage to 1960s' designer André Courrèges and the glamorous silk gowns of the 1930s and '40s.

Gwendolynne's foray into fashion began at 14, when she worked in a fabric store after school. After finishing school in Adelaide in 1988, having been named that year's best art and textiles student, Gwendolynne studied fashion design in Melbourne. She spent a decade working with some of Australia's leading fashion houses and as a pattern-maker for English fashion doyenne Katharine Hamnett. The years of hard graft paid off soon after she established her own label in 1998: she was a finalist in the Melbourne Fashion Festival's New Designer Award in 1999, 2000, 2001 and 2002.

Much of her work today is by private commission. Her sumptuously detailed garments in gossamer silks and fine laces are coveted by modern brides seeking gowns that ooze red-carpet glamour rather than traditional froufrou. "I only want to work in small quantities so I can retain the brand's value and exclusivity," Gwendolynne says. Most importantly, she wants her clothes to have longevity. Like *Phaedra*, they are likely to be admired for many years to come. *(Gwendolynne, 71 Kerr Street, Fitzroy. Full details, page 182.)* ✿

INSPIRATIONS

{ SHAG } "I find the historic range of clothing at Shag inspiring when I research different cuts and embellishment techniques. I also love the bohemian, eclectic interior." *(377 Brunswick Street North, Fitzroy, and other locations.)*

{ VIDEO BUSTERS } "I've been going here for 12 years. It has the most enormous collection of movies, which I watch for inspiration." *(134 Smith Street, Collingwood.)*

{ CAMBERWELL SUNDAY MARKET } "For its ambience and artistic treasures. My sister and I also use it to sell our old clothes." *(Station Street, Camberwell.)*

OPPOSITE: *Designer Gwendolynne Burkin is inspired by film, art and history.*

NATALIE BEGG
{ LINGERIE / FASHION DESIGNER }

Inside Natalie Begg's warehouse studio, a huge workbench is littered with inky screen-printing equipment, fabric scraps, paper patterns and works in progress. Lengths of plastic piping, around which silk will be wrapped for tie-dyeing in the Japanese *shibori* style, are propped against a wall. It seems implausible that from this apparent chaos could emerge the wispy French lace bras, daringly brief knickers and silky slips for which Natalie has made her name.

Such silken garments are the realisation of a long-held dream for Natalie. Determined to have her own fashion label, at 12 she began making hair combs wrapped in printed Liberty cottons, which she sold to local retail stores, and at 16 she made her own debutante dress. Leaving school, Natalie juggled fashion and pattern-making courses with retail work and waitressing to gain the knowledge and the money required to set up a business. She launched her self-named label in 2002 with a cotton sleepwear range. But it was a small collection of hand-painted silk underwear embellished with delicate French lace that gained most attention, and Natalie knew she had found her niche.

Today, Natalie uses hand-painting, tie-dyeing and screen-printing to stunning effect in her range of lingerie, sleepwear and woollen outerwear. Bra and brief sets sell for around $150, slips for $130 and robes for $220. "I love creating beautiful things for people to feel indulgent in," says the designer. "Silk, being a luxury item that feels so gorgeous to wear, is the ultimate expression of indulgence." *(Contact and stockist details, page 182.)* ✿

INSPIRATIONS

{ QUEEN VICTORIA MARKET } "I love buying fresh produce from the specialty ethnic food stores to create cuisines from all over the world." *(Corner Elizabeth and Victoria Streets, Melbourne.)*

{ THE BEAD COMPANY OF VICTORIA } "I often make necklaces and earrings to complement pieces in my collections, or sew beads on to garments as a feature." *(336 Smith Street, Collingwood.)*

{ SMITTEN KITTEN } "Gorgeous lingerie boutique." *(Shop 6, Degraves Street, Melbourne.)*

OPPOSITE: *Natalie Begg uses hand-painting, tie-dyeing and screen-printing in her lingerie.*

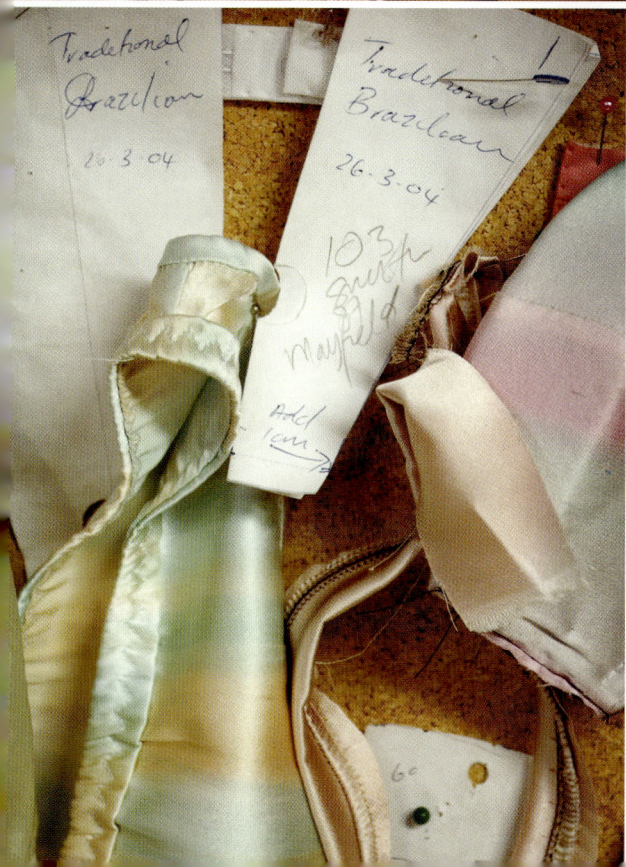

Traditional
Brazilian
26.3.04

Traditional
Brazilian
26.3.04

10¾
quilt
Mayfield

Add
1cm

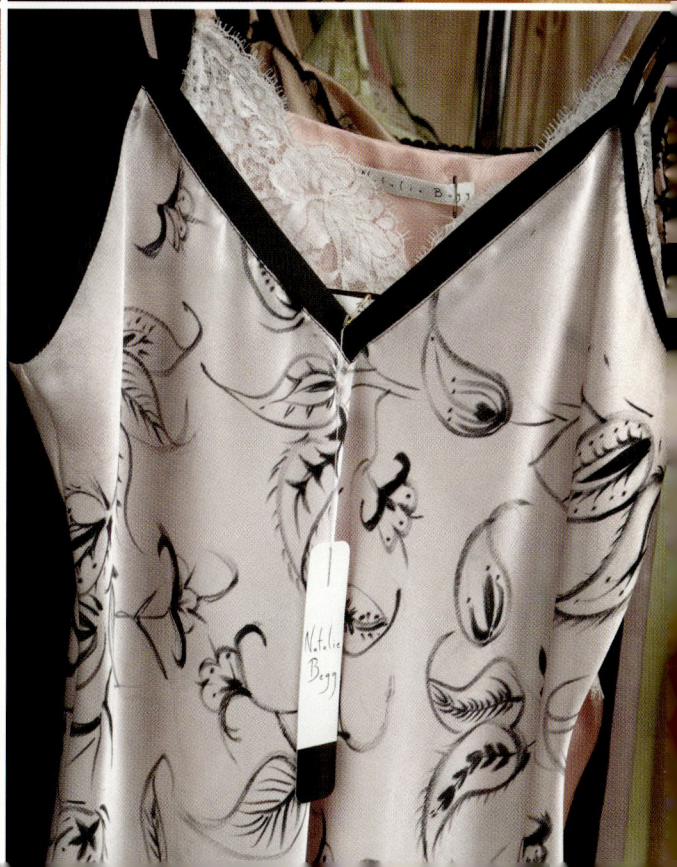

Natalie Begg

Natalie Begg

SARTI TAILORS

{ TAILORS }

Peppino Tavella's fingers are flying across a length of fabric, a small needle darting in and out as he expertly hand-stitches the soft, dark woollen cloth from which a suit will eventually emerge. Nearby stands a dummy draped in an unfinished jacket, fine chalk lines marking an adjustment here, a dart there, which will ensure it fits and flatters when its wearer slips it on.

Peppino has been a tailor most of his life. He learnt his craft in Italy, moving to Melbourne in 1964, where he worked with bespoke tailor Eugenio Niccolini. Those were heady days for the young tailor, whose customers included Australia's biggest entertainment stars – among them Bert Newton, Don Lane and the late Graham Kennedy – and leading Collins Street doctors. He met Celia Coate in 1991, when she was running a tailoring and alteration business. In 1999, they decided to meld Celia's marketing skills, eye for fine fabric and skilled styling with Peppino's tailoring mastery to establish Sarti Tailors.

A Sarti suit begins by gauging exactly what the customer wants, from fabric type and lining colour to lapel width and special requirements, such as a mobile phone pocket. Once measurements are taken, a paper pattern is made. Fabric is cut and the suit temporarily tacked for a first fitting. It is then readjusted and horsehair canvas inserted in the front to provide strength and structure. Sleeves are added and chalk is used to mark where pockets, label and lining will be placed. Another fitting is held before finishing touches, such as hand-sewn buttonholes and edges, are added.

The process takes about a week and will cost up to $4000, depending on the fabric (Celia sources from the finest European mills). "Everything about a suit like this has integrity," she says. "Customers can feel the difference immediately – it has a softer look and seems lighter to wear." *(Sarti Tailors, shop 6, 144 Little Collins Street, Melbourne. Full details, page 189.)* ✿

INSPIRATIONS

{ KAZARI COLLECTOR } "Lots of huge antique oriental and Japanese sculptures, artworks, furniture, fountains, fabulous pots and exquisite cards. There is always something you can afford, even if it is just a card." *(450 Malvern Road, Prahran.)*

{ ELLIOT SALON } "John's salon has a fabulous warehouse feel. The walls are adorned with art, the best B&O sound and video system is playing fashion parades, and of course, there is Elliot (as I call him), a mad Scot who is the best at cutting hair." *(50 Davis Avenue, South Yarra.)*

OPPOSITE: *Celia Coate and Peppino Tavella, whose suits are custom-made the old-fashioned way.*

NIKKI GABRIEL

{ KNITWEAR AND TEXTILE DESIGNER }

Fusing raw, organic materials with an ingenious eye for design, Nikki Gabriel has turned knitwear's homespun image on its head, creating sculptural garments that many view as wearable art. A self-taught knitter, Nikki made her foray into business in the early 1990s, when her small collection of knitted blankets, cushions and cosies for eggcups and latte glasses was picked up by a national homewares company.

After moving to Melbourne from Sydney in 1991 to study textile design, she began experimenting with wearable knits. Her eye-catching exhibition of lacy corset tops and diaphanous cardigans at the 2003 Mercedes Fashion Week resulted in a steady list of orders. It also caught the eye of Australian designer Akira Isogawa, with whom she collaborated on a range of raw silk and distressed cable knits, many of which were sold in Europe and Japan.

Today, Nikki works from a large inner-city studio, all whitewashed floorboards and snowy walls. In one corner are sinks where she colours yarns with natural materials – madder root, indigo, cochineal and pomegranate – and in another, bamboo scaffolding draped with drying wool.

Elsewhere sits an old knitting machine on which Nikki fashions at least half of her garments, along with a large timber table littered with spools of hand-dyed silk, cotton, linen and wool, and knitting needles of various sizes, on which she creates her chunky wraps and roll-necked cardigans. Using techniques she developed herself, Nikki "builds" her pieces without seams. Textures can be altered as she goes, by tucking or dropping stitches or by floating threads across the knit. Sometimes she adds further embellishment with print, paint or embroidery. Knitted or crocheted buttons provide the finishing touch.

"I make clothes because I love the playfulness of dressing up, of seeing what the cloth wants to do on the body and by using that to proportion the textile to work into the garment's shape." *(Contact details, page 185.)* ❧

INSPIRATIONS

{ GALLERY FUNAKI } "I love to peer into the windows of this jewellery gallery to study the textures of the treasures inside." *(4 Crossley Street, Melbourne.)*

{ ALICE EUPHEMIA } "The best platform for local (clothing design) talent. I always find something to fall in love with here." *(Shop 6, Cathedral Arcade, 37 Swanston Street, Melbourne.)*

{ HUSK } "I love the whole experience of this place, especially in winter while sipping a honeyed chai tea surrounded by oils burning, the fireplace and yummy fashion." *(123 Dundas Place, Albert Park, and other locations.)*

OPPOSITE: *Nikki Gabriel uses knitting techniques she developed herself.*

BRENDAN DWYER
{ SHOEMAKER }

At a time when the Australian footwear industry was heading into decline and manufacturing contracts were going overseas, Brendan Dwyer made his debut as a shoemaker. Almost two decades ago, he dropped out of a computer course to dabble in alternative fashion and pattern-drafting, a move that fostered his fascination with shoes.

Brendan's studio recalls a bygone time. Sweet-smelling rolls of leather and a vast collection of time-worn tools vie for space on his solid work benches. A shoe is not as simple as it looks, says Brendan, whose skills are largely self-taught. Even a seemingly straightforward pair of women's pumps takes hours to create. More ornate designs for theatrical or film productions can involve weeks of physically demanding work and up to 200 processes. Moulding leather around the last (the form that defines the shoe's shape) is particularly strenuous.

For inspiration, the softly spoken shoemaker looks to 20th century art and design, in particular Art Nouveau and German minimalism. He appreciates Northern European "fairytale" styles and admires the flamboyant clubwear designs of Canadian shoemaker John Fluevog and Briton Terry de Havilland.

Circus Oz and the Melbourne Theatre Company provide him with long-term projects that break up the familiar pattern of making one commissioned pair of shoes at a time. Brendan made much of the footwear – including complex, Spanish-inspired riding boots – for the film production of *Ned Kelly* in 2002. But he is just as happy working for clients who come to him with orthopaedic issues, in search of comfort, or simply hankering for an alternative to mainstream fashion. Prices range from $80 for a pair of simple acrobat slippers to $1500 for "some serious boot action". *(Contact details, page 184.)*

INSPIRATIONS

{ COLLECTED WORKS BOOKSHOP } "For its delight in the wordsmith."
(Level 1, Nicholas Building, 37 Swanston Street, Melbourne.)

{ MISSING LINK RECORDS } "For not being shy about music."
(Basement 405 Bourke Street, Melbourne.)

{ SPAN GALLERIES } "For the diversity of work that it shows."
(45 Flinders Lane, Melbourne.)

OPPOSITE: *Brendan Dwyer is as happy making shoes for clients seeking comfort as he is crafting exotic or historical footwear for theatre and film productions.*

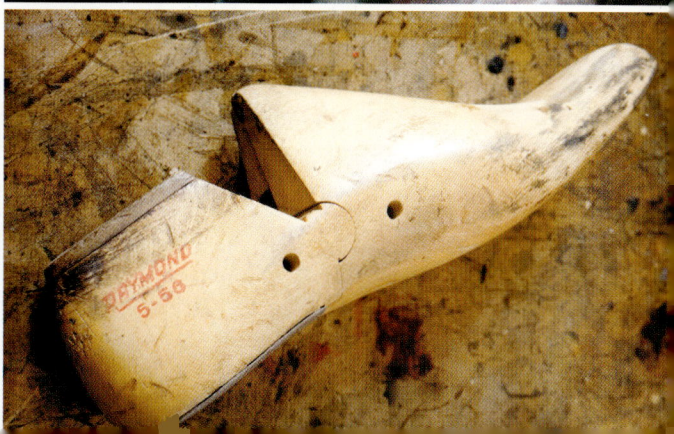

EUGENE NOTERMANS

{ SHIRTMAKER / TAILOR }

Eugene Notermans was a textile engineer with the iconic Australian fabric firm Bradmill in the 1970s when he became frustrated by the lack of interesting men's shirts available. His long arms also meant he had trouble finding shirts to fit.

So, with a pattern-maker and cutter – along with the machinist who still works with him today – Eugene opened a tailoring business with the aim of elevating the shirt from the role of understudy to the suit, to leading player in the wardrobe of any well-dressed man.

His business, Hemden Master Shirtmakers and Tailors, quickly established a reputation for producing impeccable shirts from the finest European cottons, silks and linens. Many of Melbourne's best-dressed politicians, businessmen and television personalities have come to rely on Eugene's eye for colour, shape and style when choosing dress shirts.

From a workroom behind Hemden's Armadale retail salon, a small team produces up to 100 made-to-measure shirts each week, along with hand-tailored suits. The shirt-making process begins by discussing with the client where and how the shirt will be worn. Then there is a series of decisions to be made – ranging from fabric and fit to collar and cuff style – before measurements are taken and a pattern made. With one fitting in between, the shirt will be complete within two weeks and cost $350. Subsequent shirts without a fitting cost $300.

Eugene likens his store to a men's club, where idiosyncrasies are indulged. "Men can be very particular about their shirts. Some like their buttons close together; others have a thing about their collars. We have a lot fussy customers, and we are incredibly patient with them all." *(Hemden Master Shirtmakers and Tailors, 1024-1026 High Street, Armadale. Full details, page 188.)*

INSPIRATIONS

{ EMPORIUM BOTANICA } "Uncommon botanically influenced gifts, homewares and original and limited-edition botanical artworks." *(1018 High Street, Armadale.)*

{ DAVID ATKINS DESIGNS } "Wonderful handmade cufflinks, art from Australian timber and jewellery. I admire the simplicity and tactile beauty of his designs, together with the ease of use and application." *(Contact details, page 184.)*

{ ADRIENNE MURRAY, QUILT MAKER AND PATCHWORK TEACHER } "Adrienne's work attracts not only admirers but also those who find inspiration in the purpose and usefulness of quilts and those who would like to participate in the gentle art of creative sewing." *(Patchwork on Central Park, 148 Burke Road, Malvern East.)*

OPPOSITE: *Eugene Notermans (top right) of Hemden Master Shirtmakers and Tailors.*

HEMDEN
MASTER SHIRT TAILORS
MELBOURNE

42

STEWART RUSSELL

{ TEXTILE PRINTER / ARTIST }

Silver and grey gum leaves shimmer across a tightly stretched canvas in the late-afternoon sun streaming through the windows of Stewart Russell's airy studio, housed in former stables attached to North Melbourne's historic Meat Market. Botanical designs appear frequently in Stewart's screen-printed textiles, which form the basis of the edgy Spacecraft fashion, homewares and accessories label.

The well-travelled Scotsman trained in fine arts, setting up his first screen-printing studio in Sri Lanka in the mid 1980s. Returning to the UK, he became the director of London Printworks, working with design luminaries such as Vivienne Westwood. Moving to Melbourne in 2000 with his young family, he established Spacecraft textile design studio and print workshop.

Stewart's inspirations come from a diverse range of sources. He might layer iconic images such as gum leaves with traditional designs such as those found in European damask. With an eye to contemporary art trends, he also enjoys collaborating with Australian artists such as Kate Daw and Jon Campbell. From the hand-screened textiles, five Spacecraft designers (among them Stewart's partner, Donna O'Brien), produce bed linen, cushions, clothing and bags. The clothing is sold in high-end boutiques around Australia, including at the Spacecraft flagship store in Melbourne's GPO building, as well as in the UK and Japan.

Perhaps surprisingly, some of Spacecraft's most prized works are their framed "backing cloths", canvases that cover the design table during printing, becoming heavily impregnated with printed "ideas". Once discarded, these haphazard pieces recall the 1960s work of American artist Robert Rauschenberg. "Perhaps more than any single work produced by the company, these cloths capture the energy of the studio in full flight," Stewart says. *(Spacecraft, level 1, GPO Melbourne, corner Bourke and Elizabeth Streets, Melbourne. Full details, page 189.)* ✳

INSPIRATIONS

{ GERTRUDE CONTEMPORARY ART SPACES } "The exhibition program here showcases the work of emerging artists in Melbourne."
(200 Gertrude Street, Fitzroy.)

{ SYDNEY ROAD } "Defining the contemporary cultural diversity of Melbourne."

{ THE COUNTRY WOMEN'S ASSOCIATION STAND AT THE ANNUAL ROYAL MELBOURNE SHOW } "Inspirational skills, and craft with a political agenda."

OPPOSITE: *Stewart Russell's inspiration comes from diverse sources including botanical images and Australian artists.*

GEORGIA CHAPMAN

{ FASHION DESIGNER }

By the time a Vixen garment is completed, as many as 14 people will have handled it.
From the initial stages of production, when bolts of fabric are spread over workbenches to
be screen-printed, to the final stages of detailing, when hems are hand-sewn or beading is
applied, Vixen is proudly artisan-based. And heading up the diverse team of designers, printers,
pressers, cutters, makers and finishers is Vixen co-founder Georgia Chapman.

A graduate in textile design, Georgia established Vixen when she was 21 with fellow graduate
Meredith Rowe. The pair set out to create accessories that were the antithesis of throwaway
seasonal items. Their hand-printed scarves and sarongs quickly gained a following.
With Meredith's departure from the company in 2000, Georgia was joined by her current
design partner, Maureen Sohn, who has helped the brand evolve into a sophisticated fashion and
homewares label with a fiercely loyal clientele.

Inside Vixen's Fitzroy studio, sensual fabrics – silks, jerseys and velvets – are dyed, overdyed,
etched and embellished with designs influenced by Chinese paper cuts, traditional Japanese
woodblock prints and Indian beading. Eventually, the Vixen team will turn the fabrics into
clothing, accessories, cushions, quilts and lampshades. Georgia cites the intricate fabrics and
sensuous, flowing dresses of Spanish designer Mariano Fortuny as a key influence.
Like Fortuny, Vixen garments are regarded as being kind to the natural shape of a woman's
body. Georgia remains devoted to the concept of hand-crafting garments and accessories, which
many fashion commentators describe as works of art. No surprise, then, that the studio's work
has been exhibited at Sydney's Powerhouse Museum, Melbourne's SPAN Galleries and at the
National Gallery of Victoria. *(Contact and stockist details, page 183.)*

INSPIRATIONS

{ THE BEAD COMPANY OF VICTORIA } "I've always collected beads and made
accessories." *(336 Smith Street, Collingwood.)*

{ PRESTON ZLY DESIGN } "Beautiful handmade shoes that I'm addicted to.
Their product is very labour-intensive. I relate to what they are doing."
(Rear 219 Smith Street, Fitzroy; see also page 16.)

{ KOZMINSKY JEWELLERY AND ART } "When our studio was nearby, I used to
walk past every day coveting the intricately designed estate pieces and imagining the
history of the artisan and the wearer." *(421 Bourke Street, Melbourne.)*

OPPOSITE: *Vixen founder Georgia Chapman (top right); former staffer
Wendy Taylor-Roberts (bottom left) and Vixen team member
Peter Curnow screenprinting fabrics in the Fitzroy studio.*

ADORNMENT

JEWELLERY
BAGS
HATS
ACCESSORIES

MASAKO SHIBATA
{ TEXTILE ARTIST }

JULIE FLEMING
{ MILLINER }

MARY ODORCIC
{ JEWELLER }

KATE BOULTON
{ BUTTON MAKER }

FIORINA GOLOTTA
{ JEWELLER }

BRENDAN O'KEEFE
{ EYEWEAR DESIGNER }

KATE TUCKER
{ TEXTILE / HANDBAG MAKER }

MELISSA JACKSON
{ MILLINER }

LYNLEY TRAEGER
{ JEWELLER / WALKING STICK MAKER }

JULIA DeVILLE
{ JEWELLER / TAXIDERMIST }

ADRIAN LEWIS
{ JEWELLER }

MOYA DELANY
{ FASHION ACCESSORIES DESIGNER }

CAMILLA GOUGH
{ JEWELLER }

RICHARD NYLON
{ MILLINER }

MARCOS DAVIDSON
{ JEWELLER }

MATT THOMSON
{ BAG MAKER }

ILKA WHITE
{ WEAVER AND TEXTILE DESIGNER }

MASAKO SHIBATA

{ TEXTILE ARTIST }

To Masako Shibata, unpicking the stitches of a vintage kimono reveals far more than a swathe of fabric from which to fashion one of her delicate bags. To her, every kimono tells a story. Who, she ponders, might have owned the crumbled tissue found tucked into the sleeve of one? And do the finely stitched patches on another hint at a much-loved and well-worn garment?

Masako grew up in Japan, the daughter of an artisan mother who studied kimono history and traditional textile arts. She developed a lifelong love of this stately costume. After years spent in the Middle East and South-East Asia, Masako settled in Melbourne in 1999, where she decided to merge her love of the kimono with her interest in sewing to create a small collection of bags under the Shima Blue label. She presented some examples of her design – a long handle on one side loops through a shorter one opposite to create a one-handled pouch that is slipped over the wrist – to a few boutiques and was thrilled when all saw the bags' commercial potential.

Masako travels regularly to Japan, scouring second-hand shops and markets for the increasingly rare vintage kimonos. Each is then carefully unstitched and the hand-printed fabric tenderly washed and repaired, before being reworked into small bags, obi sashes, brooches, drinks coasters and *noren* (hanging fabric screens). Driven by a desire to find harmony between traditional and modern design, Masako says she hopes that connection is recognised and respected by those who own her work. *(Shima Blue, 19 Bendigo Street, North Melbourne. Full details, page 190.)* ❀

INSPIRATIONS

{ MADE IN JAPAN } "A beautiful shop with a wide variety of Japanese textiles, papers and ceramics." *(260 Collins Street, Melbourne, and other locations.)*

{ LUFT } "A fantastic boutique that showcases clothes, bags, homewares, stationery, toys and gifts with a real eye for modern aesthetics." *(212 St Georges Road, Fitzroy North.)*

{ KOKO BLACK } "The best chocolate in Melbourne. We all need our indulgences." *(Shop 4, Royal Arcade, 335 Bourke Street, Melbourne, and other locations; see also page 162.)*

OPPOSITE: *Masako Shibata scours Japanese second-hand shops and markets for vintage kiminos from which to fashion her unusual creations.*

JULIE FLEMING

{ MILLINER }

Julie Fleming's deliciously girly hats are as much a part of Melbourne's Spring Racing Carnival as the horses. Months before hooves hit turf, the city's stylish set starts flocking to her studio, frocks in tow, so Julie can work her millinery magic.

In the late 1980s, Julie spent two years training under leading British milliner Philip Somerville, whose work has crowned the heads of Queen Elizabeth II and Diana, the late Princess of Wales. She was drilled in traditional methods by women in their 70s and 80s, many of whom had been milliners since they were 14. It proved a solid grounding for her own business, which she established on her return to Melbourne in 1989.

Julie's creations fuse time-honoured methods such as hand-blocking and rolled edges, with innovative designs that recall the elegance of the 1940s and '50s. A stitched silk hat might take up to a week to complete, each layer pulled and stitched into the next to gradually form the structure. Each stage must be perfect if Julie is to achieve the correct final shape, and only then can she add the final flourish of feathers, flowers, netting or beads. The result, she says, is an item that declares to the world "I'm beautiful". A bespoke hat can cost up to $1200.

Like her Hawksburn shop, converted from an Edwardian house, Julie's boudoir-style workroom recalls a more genteel era. Most of her creations are completed on a trusty 1950s Singer sewing machine, presided over by her favourite muse, a 1930s porcelain mannequin bust on whose well-worn head she trials most designs. (*Julie Fleming Melbourne, 456 Malvern Road, Hawksburn. Full details, page 185.*) ✾

INSPIRATIONS

{ CAMBERWELL SUNDAY MARKET } "I love adding to my collections – Italian glass, milk glass, brandy balloons and china swallows. I'm determined to have china swallows flying all the way down my hallway." (*Station Street, Camberwell.*)

{ ABBOTSFORD SALVATION ARMY FAMILY STORE } "Quirky finds include a favourite giant plant pot, hand-covered in hundreds of shells." (*81 Victoria Crescent, Abbotsford.*)

{ NATIONAL GALLERY OF VICTORIA INTERNATIONAL } "To be inspired by other artists' work." (*180 St Kilda Road, Melbourne.*)

OPPOSITE: *Julie Fleming uses time-honoured techniques to make her hats, which she then embellishes with feathers, flowers, netting or beads.*

MARY ODORCIC

{ JEWELLER }

Nature provides jeweller Mary Odorcic with her greatest inspiration. The fine veins on a leaf, a bottlebrush flower's delicate stamen or native flowers gathered near a beach might influence or even become embedded in her work.

Long coils of silver wire form the genesis of each new piece. Mary cuts and twists small sections into rings, then solders them together. She hammers each ring into a flattened disc before linking rings together in chains or with fine threads of coloured silk, punctuated by unexpected treasures such as pastel-hued pearls or small chunks of resin. A closer look might reveal a tiny scrap of fabric or a dried flower suspended in the clear, solid plastic.

Always interested in art and design, Mary knew she had found her artistic niche when she chanced upon a gold and silversmithing course. While the degree focused on large-scale work, Mary says it was jewellery-making that captured her imagination. Combining part-time work with jewellery-making after leaving university, Mary exhibited her loopy silver necklaces and matching earrings, simple rings embedded with coloured resin, and delicate poppy-inspired pieces at a Mornington Peninsula winery. Buoyed by the positive response, she established her own business in 2004, and now devotes her time to producing her raw but elegant pieces. Mary's circular-looped necklaces sell for about $230, while a set of three rings is around $300.

"My work and style has gradually evolved over time, but my inspiration – that of nature's textures, shapes and colours – has never changed." *(Contact and stockist details, page 188.)* ✿

INSPIRATIONS

{ LUSH } "I love the clothes here – I always find something to buy."
(116 Greville Street, Prahran, and 250 Brunswick Street, Fitzroy.)

{ HUSK } Chic clothing and homewares. "The store interior is just beautiful, especially the fountain wall. I also enjoy a coffee sitting outside in the lovely courtyard." *(557 Malvern Road, Toorak, and other locations.)*

OPPOSITE: *Jeweller Mary Odorcic is inspired by the textures, shapes and colours of nature.*

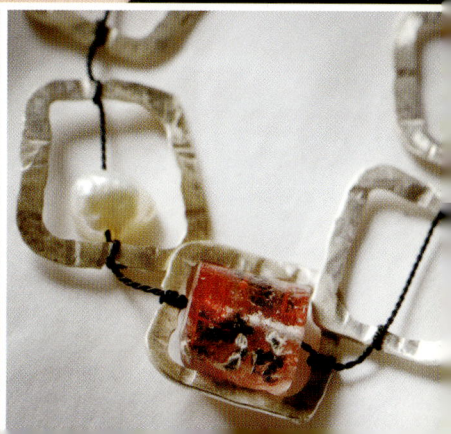

KATE BOULTON

{ BUTTON MAKER }

Kate Boulton takes pieces of rich taupe-coloured satin and nubbly bouclé and, using a cutting machine, deftly punches out a series of circular shapes. She places a circle of each fabric into a button-making die, adds cardboard and metal backing and, with the sharp pull of a lever, presses the components together. Releasing the handle, Kate carefully removes the completed button. This button, and others like it, will soon travel from her CBD studio to Sydney, where it will be sewn on to a couture garment before making a journey down the catwalk at a Collette Dinnigan fashion parade.

A lifelong button collector ("I've always loved the different colours of buttons – they're such happy things") and dressmaker, Kate was frustrated by the lack of interesting buttons available to finish her garments, so she began making her own. Realising that others must share her frustration, Kate started her button-making business, Buttonmania, in 1995. Now she makes up to 2000 buttons by hand a week and sells new and vintage buttons to artists, home dressmakers, fashion and costume designers. Kate's advice is keenly sought : her knack for picking the perfect size, colour and style of button to finish a garment is legendary.

Her city studio is crammed with the accoutrements of her trade – 100-year-old button dies and cutting machines; shelves lined with boxes of components; bags of fabric; and exercise books recording client orders, each accompanied by a fabric swatch. Dominating the space is a 200-drawer dresser, salvaged from a now-defunct button shop in Sydney's Strand Arcade, which houses her collection. Since buttonmania gripped her in childhood, Kate has amassed around two million examples – amethyst toggles from Korea and a 2000-year-old bronze Roman toga pin are among her favourites. So exhaustive is Kate's collection that much of it is now stored in a second room, which she hopes one day to transform into a button museum.

(Buttonmania, level 2, Nicholas Building, 37 Swanston Street, Melbourne. Full details, page 182.) ✤

INSPIRATIONS

{ R J HARVEY & CO } "This family-run business has been trading in tailoring supplies since 1895." *(Level 3, 37 Swanston Street, Melbourne.)*

{ ASSIN } "This eclectic fashion boutique is run by two sisters who are not afraid to break or stretch a few fashion rules." *(Basement 138 Little Collins Street, Melbourne.)*

{ FIONA ROBERTS } "Fiona makes exquisite Dorset buttons, replicas of those done in the 1880s." *(Fiona Roberts' buttons are sold through Buttonmania.)*

OPPOSITE: *Kate Boulton's studio is dominated by a 200-drawer button dresser salvaged from a Sydney shop; a button-making 'die' (top left).*

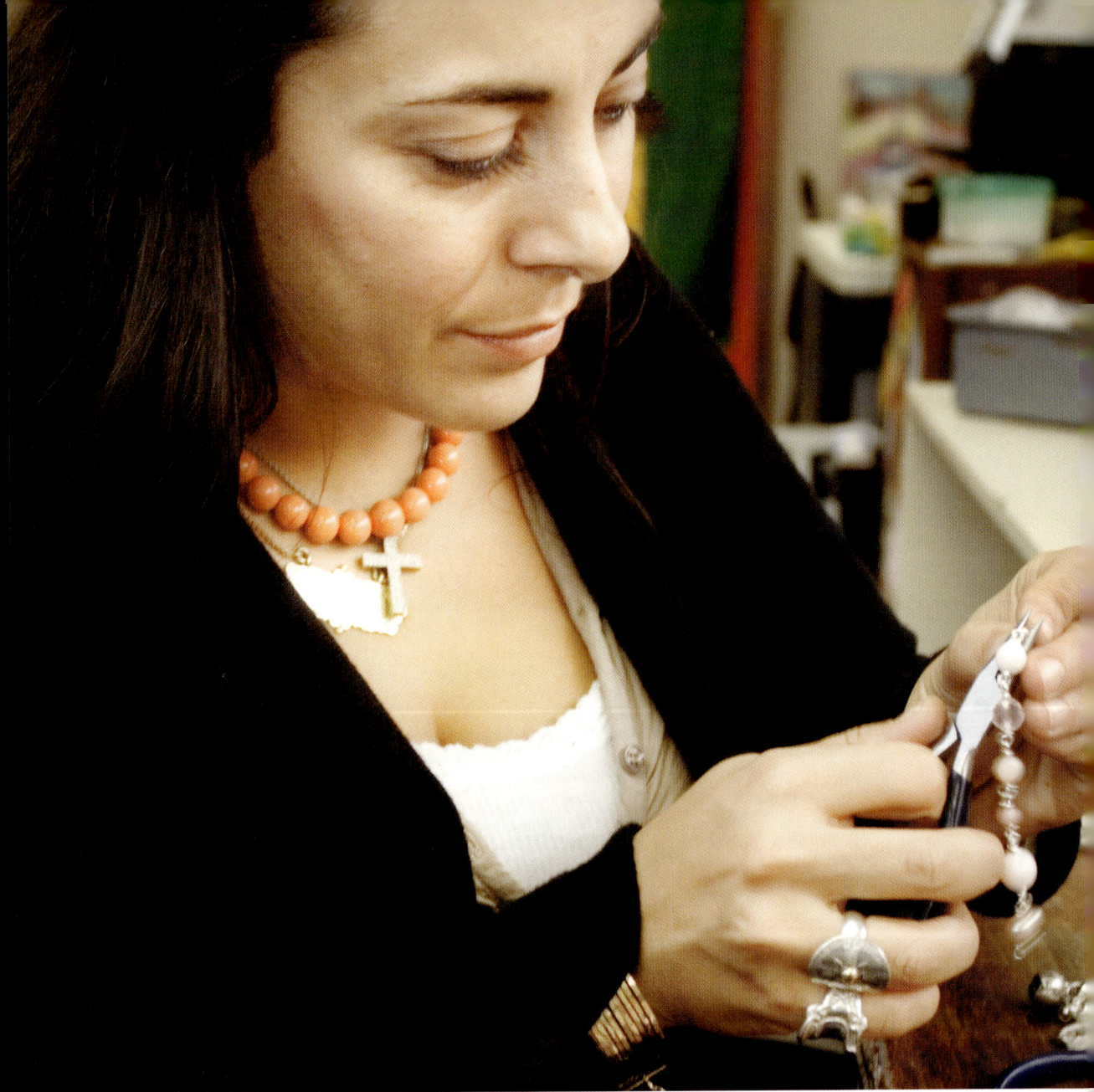

FIORINA GOLOTTA

{ JEWELLER }

To some, a florin is nothing more than an old coin. But as Fiorina Golotta turns the silver two-shilling piece over in her fingers, she sees potential jewellery. She might bend the florin gently to create a ring, add it like a charm to a long rope of sterling silver, or join it to a jangling bracelet alongside semi-precious stones such as jade, amethyst or smoky quartz.

Fiorina has been besotted since childhood with coin-collecting and jewellery-making. It seemed like a natural progression to combine the two. A decade ago, while working in fashion retail, she began making coin-based jewellery for family members and friends in her spare time. Heartened by positive feedback, she began selling her work at the (now defunct) Chapel Street Market. Her jewellery immediately resonated with those looking for timeless pieces that transcended fashion.

The self-taught jeweller is forever looking for interesting coins to include in her work, raking through pawn shops, asking travellers to scour overseas markets and imploring collectors to part with their treasures. The resulting pieces might feature a 2000-year-old Greco-Roman gold coin, a paper-thin 600-year-old Turkish piece, or a humble Australian thruppence, any of which might have passed through thousands of hands before reaching Fiorina's. The jewellery, which has an almost tribal feel, ranges in price from $250 to $2000.

"There's something very sentimental about coins," says Fiorina. "They are like talismans that can be passed from generation to generation." *(Contact details, page 185.)* ❋

INSPIRATIONS

{ THE GREVILLE STREET BOOKSTORE } "I love the contemporary and popular culture books here – they can be a real influence on my work." *(145 Greville Street, Prahran.)*

{ T L WOOD } "Exquisite clothing store that supports local artists." *(216 Chapel Street, Prahran.)*

{ CENTRAL STATION RECORDS } "Run by knowledgeable staff with a true passion for music that is not mainstream." *(2 Somerset Place, Melbourne.)*

OPPOSITE: *Fiorina Golotta has been fascinated by coins since childhood.*

BRENDAN O'KEEFE

It was a pair of wood laminate frames from France that jolted Brendan O'Keefe from eyewear retailing into design. In 1992, at a time when spectacle frames came in silver, gold or tortoiseshell, Brendan recalls being wowed by the ingenious use of wood and thinking that he could craft something equally stylish. Today, Brendan is renowned for his witty designs in boldly coloured aluminium and plastic.

At 17, Brendan began an optical mechanic apprenticeship; nine years later he had opened his own optical outlets. It soon became apparent that customers wanted more colourful and interesting frames. Brendan chanced upon the anodising process, during which aluminium is dipped into a chemical solution. When an electric current is run through the solution, the aluminium surface is coated with a coloured oxide. At the time, anodising was being used to coat door frames, windows and shower screens in black, gold or silver. But Brendan had brighter ideas. He persuaded an anodising firm to give him access to its treatment plants and, like an alchemist, Brendan dipped and dyed until he perfected the colouring technique. He then set up his own workshop, gathering frame-making equipment he made himself or bought from firms that were closing, and left retail to concentrate on design. Brendan's attention-grabbing aluminium frames – in red, orange, blue and green hues – were an immediate success.

He later expanded his range to include frames stamped from a specialised Italian plastic. The manufacturing process is labour-intensive – each pair of glasses undergoes 50 procedures before completion – so output is limited to 40 frames a week, retailing for around $400 a pair.

"I love to see people wearing my glasses," says Brendan. "It's so exciting to see what may have started as a doodle become a stylish pair of glasses." *(Contact details, page 188.)* ❧

INSPIRATIONS

{ H LEFFLER & SON LEATHER MERCHANTS} "A fascinating place selling leather, animal hides and associated products such as buckles for boots and belts." *(50-66 York Street, South Melbourne.)*

{ JENNY PIHAN FINE ART } "A wonderful gallery featuring classic paintings." *(Kananook Creek Boathouse Gallery, 368 Nepean Highway, Frankston.)*

{ ROYAL BOTANIC GARDENS MELBOURNE } "The best gardens I've seen in the world." *(Birdwood Avenue, South Yarra.)*

OPPOSITE: *Each pair of glasses that Brendan O'Keefe makes undergoes 50 procedures before completion.*

KATE TUCKER

{ TEXTILE / HANDBAG MAKER }

Kate Tucker finds inspiration for her handbags in the most unexpected places, from a city skyline wreathed in pollution to the colourful, stylised images of indigenous art.

The illustrator and multimedia designer started making bags in 2004, when she found that working at a computer all day left her creatively unsatisfied. Combining her graphic design expertise with a passion for fabrics, she produced a stylish collection of screen-printed and embroidered bags under the Katarzynkha label (a family nickname, derived from a Polish form of Kathryn).

Creativity has surrounded Kate all her life. Her grandmother taught her to sew simple bags and clothes using her mother's collection of vintage fabrics and beads, an artist aunt encouraged her to draw, and her father was a photographer. It seemed inevitable, says Kate, that she would end up working with her hands.

Kate's collection features everyday bags made from fabric and leather as well as ornate one-off pieces featuring digitally printed fabrics on to which pictures are hand-embroidered. Kate designs the fabrics on computer, transferring the images to cotton or hemp using digital technology or traditional screen-printing. She then sews the bags together, adding charms and embellishments. Purses start at $39, handbags range from $149 to $329, and one-off pieces vary in price, depending on the work involved.

Kate likes to think of her bags as wearable art. "When we think of a product more as art and less as something to be thrown away, we can really value it and let it enhance our lives."
(Contact and stockist details, page 191.) ❀

INSPIRATIONS

{ JESSIE TUCKER } "My sister, who is an underwear designer. She is an inspiration to me with her vision for both of our work, and in teaching me that people are open to something new and different." *(Contact details, page 191.)*

{ CRAFT VICTORIA } "The gallery and shop are fabulous places to visit, be inspired by, and to shop at." *(31 Flinders Lane, Melbourne.)*

{ CHAPEL STREET BAZAAR } "All sorts of wonderful objects from many different eras." *(217-223 Chapel Street, Prahran.)*

OPPOSITE: *Kate Tucker thinks of her bags as wearable art.*

MELISSA JACKSON

{ MILLINER }

Enter Melissa Jackson's studio and your eyes are drawn to an enormous barbed-wire chandelier. Its outstretched arms hold hats of every shade and shape, their frothy forms contrasting strongly with the prickly wire. The juxtaposition sits well with this accomplished milliner, who delights in a touch of the unexpected. Long strands of fishing line might replace a veil on a bridal headdress, and buttons embellish a hat where others might use feathers or flowers.

Melissa's unorthodox approach reflects a career as diverse as her designs. After completing a textile design course and a music degree, she was accepted into London's Central Saint Martins College of Art and Design in 1996, specialising in knitwear. Returning to Melbourne two years later, she started dabbling in millinery, a skill she learnt from her grandmother, a milliner who worked in Melbourne during the 1920s and '30s. Melissa's big break came when six of her designs were selected for a parade at the ultra-chic (and now defunct) George's department store in 1998. There was no looking back.

Using traditional blocks collected from markets around the world, Melissa sculpts hats from sinamay (banana plant fibre), coloured and stiffened with car spray-paint into "quite sculptural and wonky" designs. More conventional capelin and hooded styles are dyed, twisted, pleated and folded into the capricious forms beloved by Melissa's clients. Her made-to-order hats sell for between $300 and $750. Melissa's headgear is inspired by anything from a Henri Matisse painting to an early Victorian bonnet. "Each hat has its own form of expression and personality – be it wit or sophistication, tailored or quirky." *(Melissa Jackson, 195 Gertrude Street, Fitzroy. Full details, page 186.)* ❧

INSPIRATIONS

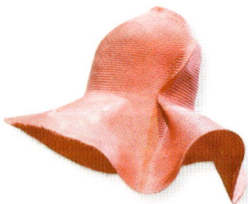

{ MY GRANDMOTHER, DOREEN JACKSON } "She taught me the traditional side of hat-making and always encouraged me to challenge convention and develop my own style. She was an eternal optimist and a unique individual."

{ QUEEN VICTORIA MARKET } "A place with incredible energy and enthusiasm. The fashion aisles are a great place to source things for styling jobs and find bargains for myself, such as my $25 hot-pink vinyl biker jacket! People often ask 'Did you buy that in Paris?' " *(Corner Elizabeth and Victoria Streets, Melbourne.)*

{ SHOREHAM, MORNINGTON PENINSULA } "A wonderful place to rejuvenate and relax among its rolling green hills, eucalypts and pines. It inspires and nurtures my imagination."

OPPOSITE: *Melissa Jackson learnt traditional millinery skills from her grandmother, although her hats may feature unconventional touches.*

LYNLEY TRAEGER

{ JEWELLER / WALKING STICK MAKER }

Inspiration can strike under the strangest circumstances. Walking to work one day in 1999, gold and silversmith Lynley Traeger was hit by a car, an accident that left her permanently in need of a walking aid. Disappointed by the unsightly walking sticks available, Lynley started dreaming of a stick that would be beautiful as well as functional.

Already an expert jeweller, for some time Lynley had been yearning to create larger-scale works. But until the accident, she had no idea what. Her first stick – borne of necessity and still used every day – was made from bamboo and topped with a vintage goat's horn umbrella handle. "I made this stick because I didn't want to walk around on crutches. But then came the thud of realisation that this object contained all my aesthetic values – and new opportunities," she recalls. Lynley's eclectic sticks, staves and walking canes evoke images of King Arthur, wizard Gandalf from *The Lord of the Rings* and Darth Vader's light sabre. Using laser precision-cutting and hydraulic press tooling, Lynley combines high-tech materials such as titanium and stainless steel with organic materials such as gnarled bamboo grown in friends' backyards.

Other sticks are all-metal, overlaid with snakeskin-like steel mesh or copper and titanium links. These technically masterful, repetitively linked structures have long featured in Lynley's jewellery, which she still makes on commission. She has found immense satisfaction in making utilitarian walking sticks more desirable. "I subscribe to the idea of creating a higher ritual out of a common habit." *(Contact details, page 190.)* 🦋

INSPIRATIONS

{ C H SMITH MARINE } "I love this fishing tackle shop. There are lots of interesting objects – nets, strings, stainless steel bits and pieces – that are used in the aggressive, corrosive environment of the sea." *(16 Langridge Street, Collingwood.)*

{ GALLERY FUNAKI } "This is a gallery that continues to challenge the preconceived perceptions of what jewellery can be. An intimate space that is successful and committed to its cause." *(4 Crossley Street, Melbourne.)*

{ CITY LIBRARY } "Because it is such a powerful space with so much opportunity to learn and research." *(253 Flinders Lane, Melbourne.)*

OPPOSITE: *Lynley Traeger combines high-tech metal with materials such as gnarled bamboo to make her walking sticks; the decorative cake cover (bottom right) is a one-off larger piece featuring hand-made chain mail links, an emu egg and feathers.*

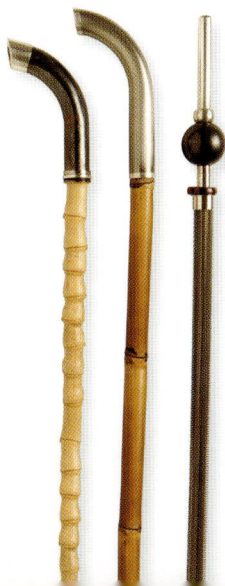

JULIA deVILLE

{ JEWELLER / TAXIDERMIST }

Julia deVille brings new meaning to the term "morbid fascination". Combining the craft of taxidermy with jewellery-making, she produces pieces that are at once confronting and intriguing. A sense of death pervades her home and studio, but in a respectful and unexpectedly elegant way. In the converted garage where she works, a stuffed wax-eye bird with a tiny diamond for its eye lies curled in a foetal position among her tools. In Julia's living room, a vintage rat trap serves as a whimsical sculpture alongside a display of human skulls, while mounted behind glass on one wall are the black beaded sleeves of a Victorian mourning dress.

Completing a diploma in gold and silversmithing after fashion and footwear design studies on both sides of the Tasman, the New Zealand-born designer developed an interest in the *memento mori* ("remember that you must die") jewellery of the 15th and 16th centuries.

Skulls and crossbones – traditional symbols of death – feature prominently among Julia's brooches, bracelets, rings, necklaces and fob chains, made under the Disce Mori label. Prices range from $320 for a silver crossbones brooch to $10,000 for specialised hand-made pieces. Jet, a petrified wood used in mourning jewellery during Queen Victoria's reign, is a favourite material and she also works with human hair, vintage ivory, diamonds and rubies. But it is her use of dead animal parts – stuffed or used to make moulds for metal-casting – that gives Julia's jewellery its special resonance. She is emphatic that she would never kill an animal for her craft: most specimens are donated by friends who stumble across recently deceased mice, birds or possums.

Some find her work gruesome but Julia enjoys challenging their views of death. "Dead animals are used every day in many ways but most people don't like to think about it. Why is one dead animal more confronting than another?" The 20-something designer's aim is to remind us that we are all mortal. "It's not meant to be morbid," she says. "It's about reminding us of the fragility of life." *(Contact and stockist details, page 184.)* 🐾

INSPIRATIONS

{ INDUSTRIA } "Fantastic industrial furniture and objects. It's worth the visit just to meet the owners, Sue and Quenton." *(202 Gertrude Street, Fitzroy.)*

{ KEYHOLE ENGRAVING CO } "The only good hand engraver I have found in Melbourne." *(Shop 16a, Port Phillip Arcade, 232 Flinders Street, Melbourne.)*

{ SMITTEN KITTEN } "Beautiful hand-made lingerie and accessories with an emphasis on local designers. Everything a girl could want." *(Shop 6, Degraves Street, Melbourne.)*

OPPOSITE: *Julia deVille aims to remind us that we are all mortal.*

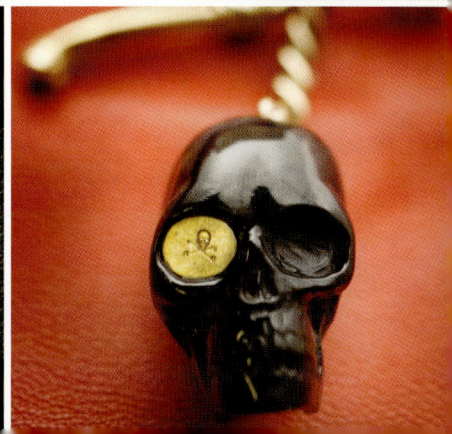

ADRIAN LEWIS

{ JEWELLER }

Adrian Lewis's elegant, refined style is evident from the front window of his Toorak Road boutique. Peering past a single, sparkling 60-carat aquamarine ring artfully suspended in a floating white cube, the only sign of clutter inside the starkly minimalist store is Adrian's immaculately groomed Staffordshire bull terrier, Gus. "Less is more" has always been Adrian's mantra. "I like the idea of taking just one thing, but an absolutely fabulous thing," he says.

Born in England, Adrian wanted to be a jeweller from the moment he set eyes on the crown jewels while visiting the Tower of London as a seven-year-old. His childhood interests – history, heritage and colour – continue to inform his work today.

Moving to Australia at 16, Adrian served a jewellery apprenticeship in Melbourne before relocating to Sydney, where his contemporary take on classical jewellery soon garnered attention. His jewellery hit the right note with performers Kylie Minogue, Grace Jones and Marcia Hines, and has featured in the fashion collections of Collette Dinnigan and Wayne Cooper. Back in Melbourne since 1991, Adrian works with two assistants in a small, orderly workroom above his store. Much of his work is custom-made, each piece involving several consultations with the client.

His jewellery is defined by colour and scale and inspired by nature. "It's never about value," he says. Precious diamonds and pearls, for instance, might be combined with less expensive stones, ebony or coral. His four-claw gem rings look equally chic with jeans or a ball gown. Such versatility is a common theme in Adrian's work. The diamond-encrusted clasp on a coral necklace, for instance, can be removed and worn separately as a brooch.
(Adrian Lewis, 29a Toorak Road, South Yarra. Full details, page 187.) ✿

INSPIRATIONS

{ CHRISTINE } This basement-level boutique is "a jewel box of wonderful things". *(181 Flinders Lane, Melbourne.)*

OPPOSITE: *Adrian Lewis's mantra is 'less is more'.*

MOYA DELANY

{ FASHION ACCESSORIES DESIGNER }

Strolling along a New York street in the late 1990s, Moya Delany was accosted by Deborah Harry, of Blondie fame, who wanted to know where she could buy black feathered angel wings like the ones on Moya's back, which she had made herself. Motivated by the new wave diva's enthusiasm, Moya walked into the influential New York boutique Bond 07 by Selima with examples of her work and promptly received a commission to create a range of feathered accessories and cocktail headpieces.

Now back in her home town, Moya often works into the night at her small inner-city studio, creating men's and women's fashion accessories and homewares such as lampshades and decorative wall pieces. Feathers – "exotic, tactile and real" – remain a hallmark of her work, although Moya uses a broad palette of materials. Beads, leather hides, metal bindings and found objects inject a tribal mood into necklaces, wristbands, belts and headpieces. Elsewhere, she brings together silk ribbons and antique kimono fabric to make sculptural belts. For her Aztec-inspired lariat necklaces, Moya employs a traditional binding technique, winding fine cotton threads over leather straps to create wonderful striped patterns.

An obsessive gatherer, Moya treasures her collection of feathers, some found by her, others gifts from people who admire her work. She darts to a shelf and reaches for a plastic bag, pulling out two rare blue and red Macaw feathers. "Aren't they just fabulous?" she enthuses. But whatever she is working with, Moya's eye is firmly on the detail. "The finish is everything," she says. "The back has to look as good as the front." Her painstaking approach has brought wide recognition: Moya's work has been spotted on the necks of actor Sharon Stone, and musicians Bruce Springsteen and Shirley Manson. *(Contact and stockist details, page 184.)* ❋

INSPIRATIONS

{ KAZARI COLLECTOR } Contemporary Asia-Pacific art and antiques. "I love all things Japanese and Kazari has the best there is." *(450 Malvern Road, Prahran.)*

{ MUSEUM VICTORIA } "For the amazing stuffed birds and ancient Aboriginal things." *(Nicholson Street, Carlton.)*

OPPOSITE: *Moya Delany obsessively gathers fabrics, beads, ribbons and other objects for her work.*

CAMILLA GOUGH

{ JEWELLER }

Working behind the closed door of her compact city studio, Camilla Gough seems oblivious to the evening rush hour in the city streets below. By the light of a lamp retrieved from a recycling pile, she methodically hammers a piece of white gold into shape around a steel ring mandrel.

Camilla's work has been described as looking like it fell off a passing aircraft. Not that she minds – the energetic jeweller strives for a strong industrial edge. Her rings, in particular, evoke tiny cogwheels or small communication devices such as might be seen in a science fiction movie. But despite the assembly-line allusions, every component of Camilla's work is wrought by hand from silver, white and rose gold, titanium and platinum, some decorated with precious stones. Camilla seldom draws her designs before she begins work, preferring to allow each piece to evolve. Some pieces take a few hours to complete, others many days.

A jeweller for the past 12 years, having fallen into the trade soon after leaving college, where she studied sculpture, Camilla says she is inspired by everything around her – from the layered bill posters in nearby laneways to the "absolutely still" urban landscape she observes while riding her bike home from work at night. Her clients are another source of inspiration. "Jewellery is only bought for good reasons. It is always joyous. I'm privileged to hear gorgeous stories of love and friendship from my clients."

Camilla's work ranges from about $300 for a silver graffiti ring to several thousand dollars for a cherry blossom ring featuring pink sapphires and white diamonds.
(Contact and stockist details, page 185.) ❧

INSPIRATIONS

{ GALLERY FUNAKI } "For the craft exhibitions that sit on the edge of art and are always interesting and strong." *(4 Crossley Street, Melbourne.)*

{ TOLARNO GALLERIES } "Some of my favourite Australian artists show with this gallery and it's really local to my workshop."
(Level 4, 289 Flinders Lane, Melbourne.)

{ AUSTRALIAN CENTRE FOR CONTEMPORARY ART } "Really striking and endlessly impressive Wood Marsh building. Challenging exhibitions that I may not always like but I always walk away with a sense of having seen or heard something new." *(111 Sturt Street, Southbank.)*

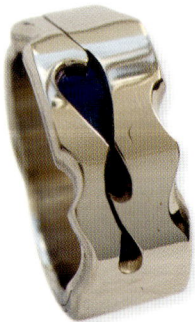

OPPOSITE: *Camilla Gough at work in her city studio.*

RICHARD NYLON

{ MILLINER }

Richard Nylon's hats are not for shrinking violets, nor for those seeking a minimalist approach. In fact, there is nothing spare about this artisan or his work: Richard wears the title "eccentric" as comfortably as he does his cravat and cheesecutter cap. The self-taught milliner likes to challenge convention. Once asked to create a hat entirely of Tupperware, he cut and remodelled the plastic containers into a flock of swooping bluebirds.

As a fashion design student in the 1980s, Richard often made headgear to match his own clothes. His sartorial flair caught the eye of the now defunct Fashion Design Council, which asked him to contribute to its young designer parades. Collaborating with Melbourne fashion designer Gwendolynne Burkin *(see page 24)* on hats for her first collection in 1998 was a turning point. Their partnership endures today, with Richard describing his hats as "full stops" to her designs.

His studio is crammed with boxes of baubles, beads and trims, and shelves stacked with hat blocks cast from everyday items such as rubbish-can lids, flower pots and dome-shaped serving dishes. From this tiny cubbyhole emerges hats that take on all manner of personalities – from whimsical and fanciful to incredibly sleek and stylish. Inspired by the work of acclaimed Irish milliner Philip Treacy and England's Stephen Jones, Richard also draws on the beauty of nature to produce pieces that seem to defy gravity.

Depending on the level of detail involved, a hat may take minutes or weeks to complete. Most are commissioned by race-goers for Melbourne's Spring Racing Carnival.
(Contact and stockist details, page 188.) ❧

INSPIRATIONS

{ PRESTON ZLY DESIGN } "I have several pairs of Petr and Johanna's shoes – their workmanship is so highly skilled and the shoes are just wonderful."
(Rear 219 Smith Street, Fitzroy; see also page 16.)

{ GWENDOLYNNE STUDIO } "It's a lovely space with an Art Deco atmosphere. My work looks so good in there that I want to do my best to reflect it."
(71 Kerr Street, Fitzroy.)

{ ST PATRICK'S CATHEDRAL } "Sometimes I sit here with my Walkman playing sacred music and imagine I'm listening to an invisible choir and orchestra."
(Corner Gisborne Street and Cathedral Place, East Melbourne.)

OPPOSITE: *From his tiny studio, Richard Nylon produces hats with all manner of personalities, from whimsical to sassy.*

MARCOS DAVIDSON

{ JEWELLER }

Marcos Davidson's cosy seventh-floor city studio tells the story of an exuberant hunter-gatherer. Walls are hung with paintings by artist friends and shelves and benches are crammed with curios, among them poisoned arrow-tips, fossilised dinosaur droppings, Tang Dynasty funerary vases and a dressage helmet. "It's almost enough to make your hair stand on end," says the goldsmith and jeweller with a guffaw, adding more seriously that the treasures serve as a reference library. "They are muses for the ongoing process of creation – all jewellery is talismanic by nature."

The first child of a family with connections to the Kalgoorlie goldfields, Marcos was apprenticed to one of Melbourne's best-regarded jewellers, Lazlo Puzsar, at 14. Surrounded by "consummate craftsmen" who had arrived in Melbourne from post-war Europe, he studied silver and goldsmithing part-time before opening his first workshop in the Block Arcade in 1979. Youthful and charismatic, Marcos quickly became a darling of the fashion set, collaborating with high-profile designers of the 1970s and '80s, among them Prue Acton, Sara Thorn, Martin Grant and Jenny Bannister.

Ensconced in Elizabeth Street's Carlow House since 1990, Marcos now works exclusively on commission and his striking works have been exhibited in the city's top jewellery houses and galleries. The master stone-setter, engraver, polisher and alloy-maker relishes every step of the jewellery-making process. He also enjoys working closely with clients, many of them fellow artisans, designers and musicians. He describes his style as Neo-Phoenician – his beaten gold rings, in particular, look like antiquities from an ancient world. Bakelite, one of the earliest forms of plastic, is a characteristic feature of his work, employed with as much finesse as gold, titanium, coral and gems. *(Room 7, Level 7, Carlow House, 289 Flinders Lane, Melbourne. Full details, page 184.)* ❧

INSPIRATIONS

{ UNTIL NEVER GALLERY } "Street art source and coal-face product outlet." *(Level 2, 3-5 Hosier Lane, Melbourne.)*

{ E C MENZIES ELECTRICAL } "A mad warehouse of proto-plastic: Bakelite, Teflon and a queer range of rubber materials." *(19 Ewing Street, Brunswick.)*

OPPOSITE: *Marcos Davidson describes his style as 'Neo-Phoenician'.*

MATT THOMSON

{ BAG MAKER }

While studying at university in 1999, Matt Thomson hankered for a scooter-friendly shoulder bag to carry his laptop, books and mobile phone. His prototype backpack was a hit with family and friends and before long he was selling his backpacks, shoulder bags and laptop bags through craft markets and independent fashion stores.

Combining sturdy materials such as seatbelt webbing and nylon Cordura fabric (usually used for backpacks) with eye-catching prints, Matt's compartmentalised bags reflect both his respect for functionality and his interest in street culture. The versatility of hiking and outdoor equipment is another key influence for the former mechanical engineering and industrial design student.

Matt's well-ordered workspace – a studio in the Nicholas Building that he shares with three other artisans – has dramatic views of Federation Square, Flinders Street Station and tree-lined St Kilda Road. Next to his sewing machine is a neat rack of fabric samples, ranging from oriental prints in durable upholstery fabrics to recycled vinyl billboards, the latter used to complete a large order of bags for the Melbourne Film Festival.

Keen to develop his own range of hard-wearing fabrics, Matt recently collaborated with local designers to digitally reprint 1950s silk maps on to canvas. A screen-printed denim range is set to follow. For further inspiration, Matt need only step outside his studio. In the nearby stencil-strewn laneways, tiny cafe tables are crowded with young urbanites, a ready market for this up-and-coming designer's work. *(Contact and stockist details, page 190.)*

INSPIRATIONS

{ THE DANCING QUEEN } "An amazing source of fabrics, encouragement and useful information." *(327 Lennox Street, Richmond.)*

{ ROSE STREET ARTISTS' MARKET } "A wonderful collection of personalities and a truly rampant creative atmosphere." *(Saturdays, 60 Rose Street, Fitzroy.)*

{ H LEFFLER & SON LEATHER MERCHANTS } "Always something new to discover and it never fails to inspire new perspectives." *(50-66 York Street, South Melbourne.)*

OPPOSITE: *Matt Thomson's bags reflect his interest in street culture and functionality.*

ILKA WHITE

{ WEAVER AND TEXTILE DESIGNER }

Found objects – from the desert, the sea, the city and almost everywhere in between – spill from containers in Ilka White's studio in Melbourne's warren-like Nicholas Building. Tufts of camel hair, glossy red seeds and fragments of rusted tin, salvaged from the ruins of an outback station, sit in a wooden bowl. Tucked into an envelope are brilliant budgerigar feathers collected in the wild. To say that nature inspires Ilka is an understatement – this widely travelled artist seems to have studied every tiny twig or stone she has stumbled upon.

The recipient of a Churchill Fellowship in 2000 to study traditional weaving in Indonesia, India, Nepal and Bhutan, Ilka hand-produces woven and felted textiles incorporating souvenirs of her travels, as well as felt, leather, PVC, sequins and buttons. She brings a contemporary aesthetic to the traditional craft of weaving. In the past she has collaborated with fashion labels such as Scanlan & Theodore to produce hand-woven accessories. These days, her focus is on exhibition pieces for galleries such as Melbourne jewellery gallery e.g.etal.

Raised by creative parents with a self-sufficient bent, Ilka learned to sew as a child and was given her first loom at 12. She initially studied fashion but left mid-degree to complete a textile design course. "I wanted to start a step before fashion. I wanted to make cloth." Ilka's work contains surprising contrasts of colour and texture and is rich with narrative allusions. One recent collection included lyrics from her mother's songs, woven into the cloth and embroidered on to ribbon. At times she has collaborated with others to make computer-aided fabrics but she is drawn back to the culture and community of traditional textile weavers. "These are generous people. They are open and willing to share ideas." *(Contact and stockist details, page 191.)* ❀

INSPIRATIONS

{ APRILMAY } "A tiny shop with a lovely old-world feel: handknits made by local ladies, clothing with a classic finish, crocheted and cut-and-sew toys with button eyes, homewares and select bits of furniture." *(107 Scotchmer Street, Fitzroy North.)*

{ THE HANDWEAVERS AND SPINNERS GUILD OF VICTORIA } "Beautiful yarns hand-spun and dyed by their members." *(12-20 Shakespeare Street, Carlton North.)*

{ THE EMBROIDERERS GUILD OF VICTORIA } "A great library and an inspiring collection of exquisite historical embroidery and lace." *(170 Wattletree Road, Malvern.)*

OPPOSITE: *Ilka White was given her first loom when she was 12.*

HOMEWARES

FURNITURE
LIGHTING DESIGN AND LAMPSHADES
SOFT FURNISHINGS
CERAMICS
GLASSWARE
METAL, WOOD AND STONE WORK

JULIE CAINES
{ TASSEL MAKER }

MAUREEN WILLIAMS
{ GLASS ARTIST }

ANTON GERNER
{ FURNITURE MAKER }

CATHY HOPE
{ QUILTER }

JEREMY WILKINS
& STEPHEN KENT
{ FURNITURE MAKERS }

KYLE DE KUIJER
& STEPHANIE FLEMMING
{ HOMEWARES DESIGNERS }

MARK SHEIL
{ METAL ARTISAN }

GEOFFREY MANCE
{ LIGHTING DESIGNER }

WILLIAM MATTHYSEN
{ CLOCK MAKER }

FRED GANIM
{ TILE PAINTER }

CAMERON COMER
{ HOME ACCESSORIES DESIGNER / STYLIST }

BARBARA RICHARDS
{ LAMPSHADE MAKER }

CHRIS PLUMRIDGE
{ CERAMICIST }

WENDY GOLDEN
{ BASKET MAKER }

MARC PASCAL
{ LIGHTING AND CERAMICS DESIGNER }

PETER McLISKY
{ STONE CARVER }

GREG HATTON
{ FURNITURE MAKER }

SIMON LLOYD
{ PRODUCT DESIGNER }

ANNA LORENZETTO
{ LEATHER HOMEWARES DESIGNER }

VICKI MURFETT
{ SHELL ARTIST }

KRIS COAD
{ CERAMICIST }

MARK MARINATO
{ MIRROR MAKER }

ANNA CHARLESWORTH
{ METAL ARTIST }

BERN EMMERICHS
{ CERAMICIST }

ANDREW WOOD
{ WOOD WORKER }

PHILIP STOKES
{ GLASS ARTIST }

JULIE CAINES

{ TASSEL MAKER }

Julie Caines finds inspiration everywhere: in the riotous ruffle of a flamenco skirt; in tribal accessories worn by African dancers; in the severe details on a gladiator's tunic; and in the jewel-like shades of a peacock feather. This self-taught tassel maker – or *passementière* – stumbled on the venerable craft by accident. Horrified by the cost of French-made tasselled curtain tiebacks she wanted for her Victorian terrace house, Julie invoked her talent for making things – she had previously dabbled in dressmaking, weaving, embroidery, tapestry, knitting, crochet, jewellery, pottery, mosaics and leadlighting – and created her own.

To perfect her skills in passementerie – the decorative use of cording, trim and braid to create tassels – Julie took braiding lessons and spent months taking tassels apart to discover how each fused together. An acquaintance in the interior design industry spotted Julie's talent and offered to act as her agent. Today, Julie is one of only two known bespoke tassel makers in Australia. Her work is sold through interior design stores to clients ranging from discerning suburban dwellers to international hotels.

The former plastics sales manager works in solitude in her warehouse studio, surrounded by colourful spools of cotton and silk threads, boxes brimming with jewel-like beads, and baskets of intricately carved wooden forms. Julie creates her tassels by winding coloured thread around a form, decorating it with handwoven braids and skirts (fringes) and finishing it with a rope embrace. Depending on its complexity, a tassel might take anywhere from five minutes to five weeks to complete and cost between $30 and $500. *(Contact and stockist details, page 182.)* ✹

INSPIRATIONS

{ BISTRIN'S EMPORIUM } "For its eclectic mix of clothing and accessories, including some by great local designers." *(201 Gertrude Street, Fitzroy.)*

{ KANELA SPANISH FLAMENCO BAR } "I'm passionate about flamenco dancing. One of my teachers, Johnny Tedesco, teaches and performs at Kanela. I'm a late starter – it's something I've always wanted to do." *(56 Johnston Street, Fitzroy.)*

{ LAURA UHE, DANCE TEACHER } "Laura is helping me to come out of myself more. Australians tend to be more conservative in their demeanour than the Spanish, and flamenco is all attitude and passion." *(Contact details, page 191.)*

OPPOSITE: *Julie Caines spent months taking tassels apart to learn how to put them together.*

MAUREEN WILLIAMS
{ GLASS ARTIST }

Maureen Williams likens her work as a glassblower to that of a master chef. "There isn't time to play around," she says. "You've got to make quick decisions and if you make a mistake, you bin it."

Fortunately, there are not too many overflowing bins in Maureen's workplace, a long, narrow and rather spartan space on Melbourne's busy St Kilda Road.

Inspired by the Spanish ceramics and Italian glass she saw while travelling in Europe in the early 1980s, on her return Maureen threw in her job as a political secretary to begin a Bachelor of Arts.

She is now one of Australia's foremost glass artists, perhaps best known for painted vessels rich in references to her own life experiences, particularly her childhood spent in rural South Australia. Using glass as a three-dimensional canvas, she employs a complex technique to entrap paint beneath the surface of the glass and create sophisticated images. Each exhibition work takes weeks to complete; large and heavy pieces sometimes need a team of blowers to handle them in their final stages. Less challenging, but no less keenly sought, are Maureen's colourful production pieces – platters, vases, bowls – in which each colour is individually applied using a torch and tweezers. A second range, using two or three transparent colours, includes perfume bottles with distinctive party-dress shapes.

A perfectionist, Maureen accepts the need to work long hours, sometimes beginning before sunrise to take full advantage of the furnace, which remains on 24 hours a day. She lives and breathes her craft: "I want to be really good at what I do. Like a mother choosing to stay at home to care for her children, my craft needs constant nurturing. You can't cut corners but the rewards are there. It's an exciting and passionate experience."
(Contact and stockist details, page 191.) ❧

INSPIRATIONS

{ WALKING FROM ST KILDA BEACH TO MIDDLE BRIGHTON PIER }
"Contemplative and inspiring."

{ IAN POTTER CENTRE, NGV AUSTRALIA } "To study both the paintings and the painting techniques." *(Corner Russell and Flinders Streets, Melbourne.)*

{ CRAFT VICTORIA } "It's inspiring to see other people's work."
(31 Flinders Lane, Melbourne.)

OPPOSITE: *Maureen Williams (background, top left) works long hours, often starting before sunrise, to take full advantage of her 24-hour furnace; technical assistant Janeen Toner (bottom right).*

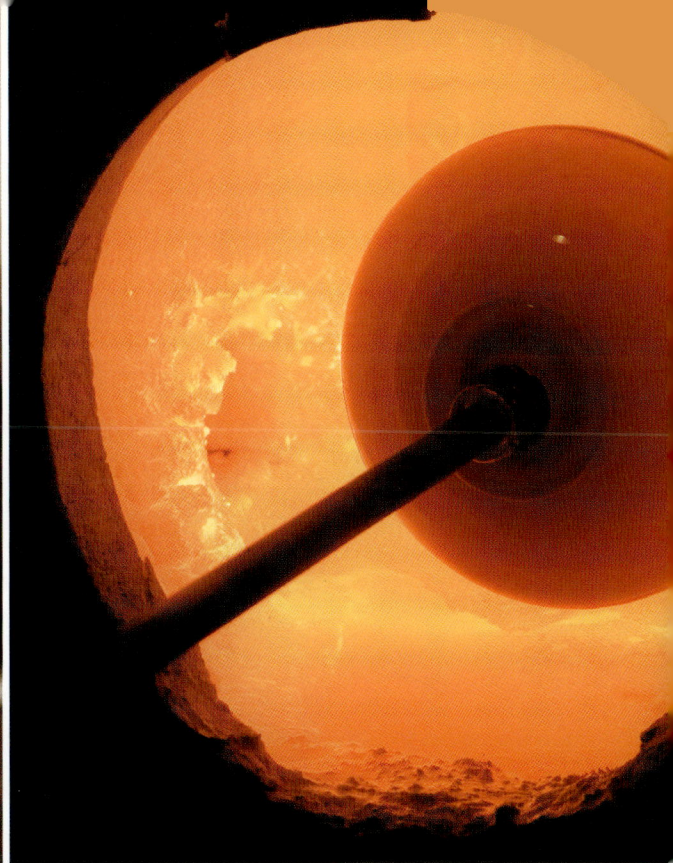

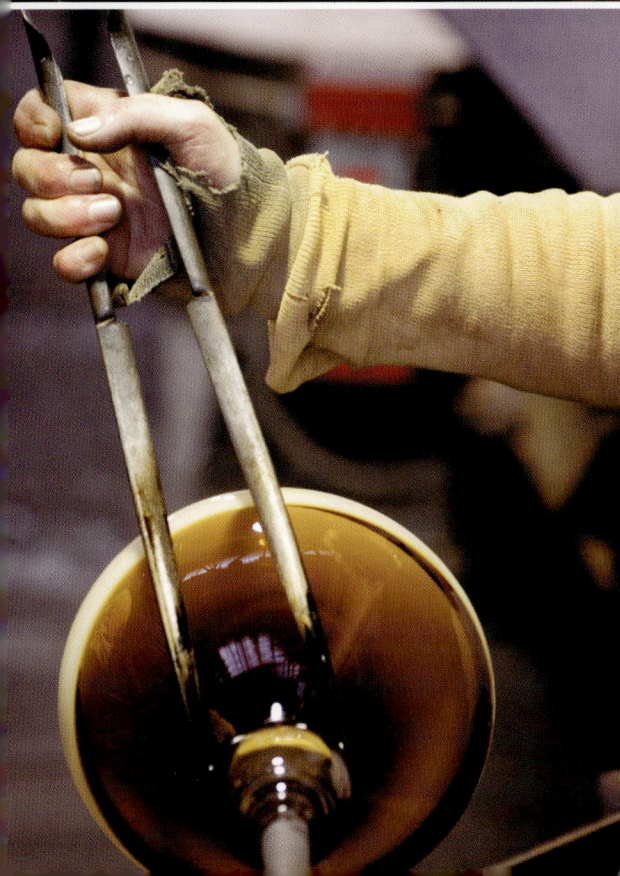

ANTON GERNER
{ FURNITURE MAKER }

Anton Gerner has never advertised. Yet he can barely keep up with commissions, such is his reputation for beautifully made furniture. The softly spoken craftsman works from a former dairy, which is usually filled with furniture in varying stages of completion, its original tiled floors littered with sawdust and wood shavings.

Classic timbers such as walnut, oak, blackwood and Australian red gum are worked into contemporary pieces inspired by the elegant, clean lines of Biedermeier and Art Deco design. Anton uses traditional tools and techniques: mortise and tenon joints, dovetails and hand-laid veneers. Many pieces feature intricate inlays and edge details and all are finished with natural oils and waxes or traditional French polishing. He produces about 10 pieces a month.

Anton was 12 when he discovered that he preferred woodwork to book work. His interest in furniture design evolved and eventually led him to a course at the Melbourne School of Woodcraft. Yet he maintains that he is largely self-taught, his skills sharpened by trial and error and ideas honed by instinct and an eye on national and international trends.

Questioned about the cost of his pieces, Anton's response is measured: a dining table might command between $3000 and $25,000, depending on the type of timber and amount of detail involved. The average price of other pieces – entertainment units are the most popular – is about $9000. *(Contact details, page 185.)*

INSPIRATIONS

{ NATIONAL GALLERY OF VICTORIA INTERNATIONAL } "I really like the exterior and have often noticed how well the stonework is done – the walls are perfectly straight and square. I also wonder if anyone else has ever noticed the 'keystone' in the archway: this is a massive piece of stone that always amazes me."
(180 St Kilda Road, Melbourne.)

{ MANCHESTER UNITY BUILDING } "My grandfather used to be a jeweller in there and I've been going there since I was young. I'm fascinated by the building, which is classic Art Deco – and a bit scary."
(corner Swanston and Collins Streets, Melbourne.)

{ GEORGE FETHERS & CO. TRADING } "They have lots of unusual and interesting veneers that you can't find anywhere else."
(216 Rouse Street, Port Melbourne.)

OPPOSITE: *Anton Gerner has sharpened his skills through trial and error.*

CATHY HOPE

{ QUILTER }

From a pile of seemingly mismatched scraps, Cathy Hope pulls out dozens of fabric squares stitched together to form a sheet. No two pieces are the same – florals sit alongside geometrics and botanical-inspired motifs butt up against richly patterned Japanese prints – yet somehow it all works. This fabulous fusion of materials marks the beginning of one of Cathy's highly sought-after quilts. From her tiny workroom strewn with cotton scraps, uncompleted works and a bench groaning with bags of material, she produces about 50 quilts a year. The workroom sits above her shop in Fitzroy, one of two owned by Cathy and her partner, Paul Douglas, which showcase their quilts and cushions as well as hand-picked clothing and accessories.

Some 15 years ago, the former textiles student had an aunt teach her traditional quilting methods. She was immediately hooked on the concept of designing and making something that would be used and enjoyed. Now, hobby has become business: Douglas & Hope offers one-of-a-kind quilts to customers ranging from serious collectors to those simply looking for a unique bedroom accessory.

Gathering a range of fabrics, including reproduction American Civil War prints and vintage kimonos, and experimenting with colour and texture (velvet is a current favourite), Cathy creates the top sheet by sewing the various pieces together. Victorian wool wadding is sandwiched between the top and a backing fabric, before the three layers are stitched together and edged with satin binding. Upholding tradition, Cathy signs and dates each quilt, a future heirloom to be passed on for generations. A single quilt can take a couple of weeks to complete and carries a $1000 price tag, yet there is a long list of customers waiting to own Cathy's contemporary take on yesteryear comfort. *(Douglas & Hope, 181 Brunswick Street, Fitzroy, and shop 4, the Block Arcade, Elizabeth Street, Melbourne. Full details, page 186.)*

INSPIRATIONS

{ HEIDE MUSEUM OF MODERN ART } "I love everything about Heide – its history, gardens and galleries." *(7 Templestowe Road, Bulleen.)*

{ CAMBERWELL SUNDAY MARKET } "Always good for a fossick. I often manage to find a few treasures." *(Station Street, Camberwell.)*

{ MIRKA MORA, MELBOURNE ARTIST } "She is an intriguing woman – her whole life has been about her art. Her work is filled with passion."

OPPOSITE: *Cathy Hope's range includes quilts and cushions.*

JEREMY WILKINS & STEPHEN KENT

{ FURNITURE MAKERS }

Stephen Kent and Jeremy Wilkins make furniture imbued with stories. Who would guess that a pair of rich, red-hued jarrah side tables were once stair treads, salvaged when Fitzroy's Gloweave factory was demolished in 1998? Or that a magnificent gleaming dining table is a reincarnation of mountain ash purlines (horizontal timbers supporting roof rafters)?

The pair's work is proof that one person's trash is another's treasure: they love nothing better than foraging through demolished homes, wreckers' yards and factories for timber that will become covetable pieces of furniture. Working from a small factory behind the showroom, they fashion wall studs, floor joists and doors into beautiful chests of drawers or small tables; red gum house stumps and railway sleepers into sideboards and bookcases; and jarrah beams into CD storage cabinets, beds and coffee tables. One customer even brought in a chest of drawers made from spotted gum to be reworked into a hall table.

Stephen and Jeremy started their business in 1994, originally to restore second-hand furniture. But in pulling pieces apart, they became fascinated by how they had originally been made. Early Australian and Depression-era furniture, crafted from need and ingenuity, still holds a special fascination. The pair's constantly evolving style is based on making pieces they would be happy to own, not on a slavish pursuit of trends. They use traditional woodworking techniques, assembling and finishing pieces by hand and applying the final gloss coat with a brush rather than a spray gun. "We like to see evidence of the human touch, rather than a mirror finish," says Jeremy. "Handmade items are all different and are more pleasing to the eye," adds Stephen. "They reflect nature because they are made by people, not machines." *(Wilkins and Kent, 230 Brunswick Street, Fitzroy. Full details, page 191.)* ❀

INSPIRATIONS

{ THE KAURI TREES IN THE ROYAL BOTANIC GARDENS MELBOURNE }
"We can't help but lick our lips at all that great timber."
(Birdwood Avenue, South Yarra.)

{ NATIONAL GALLERY OF VICTORIA AUSTRALIA AND NGV INTERNATIONAL } "They've got a huge furniture collection and it's a shame more of it isn't on display." *(Corner Russell and Flinders Streets, and 180 St Kilda Road, Melbourne.)*

OPPOSITE: *Jeremy Wilkins (top right) and Stephen Kent forage through demolished homes and wreckers' yards to find the timber they use.*

KYLE DE KUIJER
& STEPHANIE FLEMMING
{ HOMEWARES DESIGNERS }

Kyle de Kuijer and Stephanie Flemming can think of little more satisfying than seeing a row of plump cushions lined up like soldiers in a corner of their workshop. The image represents an exhaustive but productive couple of days' work for the duo behind the quirky Holly Daze homewares label. Working from a small design and print studio at the back of their home, Kyle and Stephanie draw inspiration from 1940s and '50s furniture and wallpaper and contemporary colours for their silk-screened soft furnishings.

The couple, from Castlemaine in central Victoria, moved to Melbourne in 2000, Kyle to study visual arts and Stephanie, textile design. Needing sturdy bags to carry their text books, the pair decided to collaborate on some screen-printed denim bags and when Stephanie took her bag into the homewares shop where she worked part-time and the owner loved it, a business was born.

Their whimsical, limited-edition fabric designs range from retro geometrics to detailed botanical images. Perfecting the colours for the designs is a painstaking process, says Kyle, who spends hours mixing water-based paints dollop by dollop to achieve the correct hue. They print up to six metres of fabric at a time before heat-setting the design. Then it is ready for cutting and sewing into cushions, bags, doorstops and T-shirts, which are snapped up by customers at a small range of chic clothing and homewares stores. Cushions range in price from $75 to $110 and doorstops sell for $28.

"It's a labour of love," says Kyle. "By making things ourselves we can strive for the highest standards possible, perfecting things that might otherwise get overlooked."
(Contact and stockist details, page 184.)

INSPIRATIONS

{ CRAFT VICTORIA } "A beautiful exhibition space and retail outlet for a broad and stunning range of handmade items." *(31 Flinders Lane, Melbourne.)*

{ RETRO-ACTIVE FURNITURE } "We draw a lot of inspiration and ideas from vintage items found here." *(307 High Street, Northcote.)*

OPPOSITE: *Stephanie Flemming and Kyle de Kuijer turn their limited-edition, silk-screened fabric designs into cushions, bags and doorstops.*

MARK SHEIL
{ METAL ARTISAN }

Aluminium might be better known as the stuff of drink cans, aircraft bodies and baking foil, but Mark Sheil is the second generation of his family to put it to use for beautifully crafted tableware. In the early 1960s, Mark's late father, Don, was a silversmith who began experimenting with high-purity aluminium alloy – then used mostly for cookware, shower screens and window frames – to make household items such as wine goblets, water jugs, cake stands and ice buckets. Customers fell in love with pieces that looked like silver, yet were light, functional and didn't tarnish. Joined by son Mark in 1971, the business flourished.

"My father, being creatively driven, could be very uncompromising and demanding," recalls Mark. "He would often hand me a used envelope with a scribble on it and the instructions 'Make this', and expect that a finished prototype would appear the next day. We are still finding sketch books, address books, note pads and even scraps of paper with designs and ideas, even though he passed away in 1990."

Today, a team of four produces Mark's range at a bayside workshop. Each article begins as a flat sheet of aluminium and undergoes many processes, including shaping, hand-etching, polishing and anodising, before completion. Some pieces, including wine goblets, have remained in the range since the beginning, but from time to time Mark adds new items, such as contemporary salad bowls and platters. The pieces retail from $50 to $1000.

The shapes, textures and patterns of nature inspire many of the designs (etched waratahs and flowering gum are popular motifs). Other pieces, such as sailing trophies and kitchen canisters, are created by commission.

(Sheil Abbey and Gallery, 21 Carpenter Street, Brighton. Full details, page 190.)

INSPIRATIONS

{ MELBOURNE'S PARKS AND GARDENS } "I am constantly amazed by the minds of those 150 years ago who had the foresight to create such beautiful gardens all over the city."

{ NICHOLAS DATTNER AND COMPANY } "I love the idea that old timber has been recycled into classic furniture." *(32 Gipps Street, Collingwood.)*

OPPOSITE: *Curvy wine goblets and platters etched with waratahs and flowering gum are characteristic of Mark Sheil's work.*

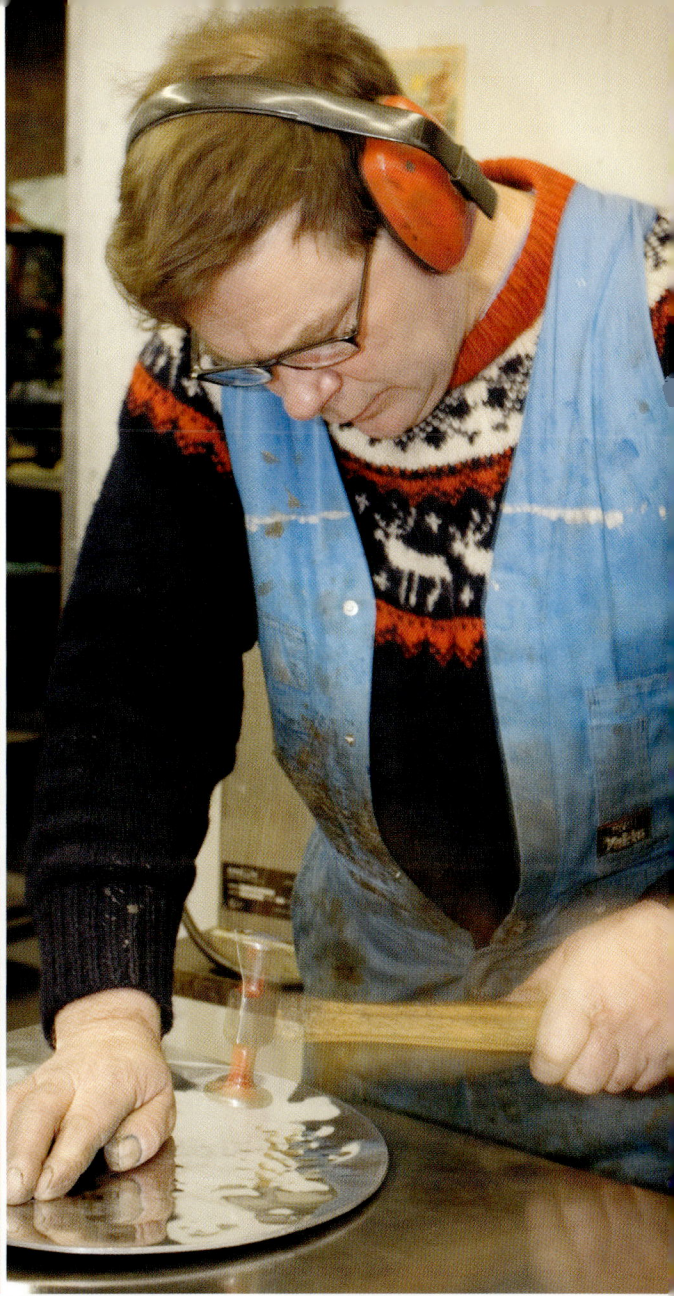

GEOFFREY MANCE
{ LIGHTING DESIGNER }

A pile of chunky logs and spindly twigs lies at the entrance to Geoffrey Mance's studio. The pile could pass for a wood stack but far from ending up as ashes, the timber is destined to become a stunning light fitting.

An electrician by trade, Geoffrey says he has always had a passion for illumination and design. Commissioned five years ago to install wall lighting at a Melbourne restaurant, he came up with the idea of using a bunch of sticks to form a shade. So positive was the response that he continued the theme for other jobs, using vines and willow branches. But it was when he stumbled across a hawthorn hedge that the concept for his successful Hedgehog light was born. The pendant shades are made by knitting dried branches together with twists of fine wire. The light glows from within and Geoffrey describes the result as "nature's disco ball". He followed this design up with what he calls Ghost Story, a shade made with pale ghost gum branches, which, when suspended from a ceiling, look like an unfinished game of pickup sticks.

Geoffrey uses fallen branches gathered with council approval from Studley Park and Yarra Bend Park, both in Kew, and materials bought from local suppliers. His Hedgehog and Ghost Story fittings, available in various sizes, can be bought in their raw state or flocked with a velvet-like fire retardant coating. A 600mm Hedgehog pendant (natural) sells for $2100 while a 1200mm Ghost Story fitting is $3300. "I'm inspired by nature as a living thing that predates and will outlive design," says Geoffrey. "Clients love that my products combine nature and lighting." *(Contact details, page 187.)* ✺

INSPIRATIONS

{ KEITH HARING MURAL } "I like it because it gives a strong message about thinking. It provides the 'why' question to me: 'Why are you here? Move or get out.' It represents to me that art can exist in an urban landscape." *(Northern Melbourne Institute of TAFE, Collingwood campus, Johnston Street, Collingwood.)*

{ EST AUSTRALIA SOAPS } "I love these handmade soaps made from olive oil, which I buy from the Red Hill Market." *(Contact details, page 184; see also page 160.)*

{ MY DOG CAFE } "My dog Ronaldo loves it too. I can buy him doggie food and he sits with me and meets other dogs with great etiquette." *(Station Pier, Port Melbourne.)*

OPPOSITE: *Hedgehog fitting (bottom right) and Ghost Story fitting (top right)*

Geoffrey Mance sadly passed away since the first release of Handmade in Melbourne, *in February 2007. The business he founded continues to trade, as Mance Design.*

WILLIAM MATTHYSEN
{ CLOCK MAKER }

William Matthysen is crafting a new clock. Not that you would guess it by looking at the partly rotten slab of wood propped against a wall of his cluttered studio. The piece of 500-year-old Huon pine, dredged from Tasmania's Huon River, will form part of one of his ingenious timepieces.

The South African-born artisan fell in love with clocks as a child, when he managed to pull apart then repair the family's broken mantel clock. He recalls a real sense of achievement in getting it to work. After studying architecture at Johannesburg's University of the Witwatersrand, William worked as an architect in Amsterdam, Hong Kong and London, moving to Melbourne in 1986. It was while studying urban design that William's interest in clocks was rekindled. "I'm passionate about them – they provide me with the means of exploring ideas about design, materials and craftsmanship and combining them into an integrated whole."

Unlike traditional clocks, where only the clock face and its case are visible, William's contemporary timepieces put the mechanism on show. Inspired by kinetic sculpture, mining poppet heads, lighthouses and the grain silos that dotted the landscape of his youth, William makes three-dimensional sketches and scaled technical drawings before building a working prototype. Satisfied that design and mechanical elements are in sync, he embarks on the clock. His dexterity with timber and metal allows him to design and make both the clock housing and most of its inner workings.

Depending on its complexity, each clock might take up to six months to complete and cost between $4500 (for a mantel clock) and $25,000 (for a 1.8-metre tall wall-mounted cabinet clock). Often described as "tomorrow's antiques", William's thoroughly modern timepieces are made mostly by commission and have been shown in galleries across Australia and overseas. *(48 Webb Street, Warrandyte. Full details, page 187.)* ✣

INSPIRATIONS

{ BRUCE JACKSON, GLASS GILDING ARTIST } "Like me, Bruce is engaged in mastering an old technique and reapplying it to the contemporary world." *(Contact details, page 186.)*

{ CARL LUTZ, FURNITURE RESTORER AND WOOD CARVER } "An established craftsman with an encyclopaedic knowledge of traditional timber finishes and carving techniques." *(Contact details, page 187.)*

{ ADAM STEWART, CONTEMPORARY FURNITURE MAKER } "A young designer producing contemporary work of the highest order." *(Contact details, page 190.)*

OPPOSITE: *William Matthysen's contemporary timepieces put the mechanism on show.*

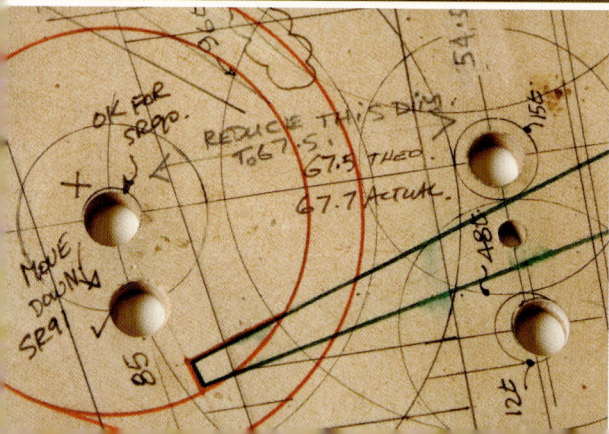

OK FOR
SR90

MOVE
DOWN
SR91

X

REDUCE THIS DIM.
TO 67.5.

67.5 THEO.

67.7 ACTUAL.

54.5

155

480

85

12t

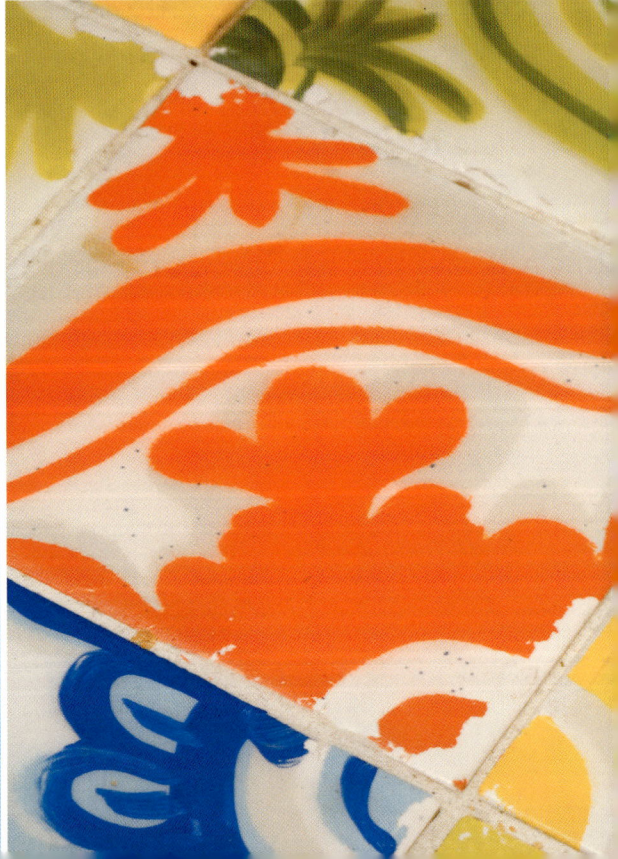

FRED GANIM
{ TILE PAINTER }

It's a long way from a mosaic-tiled stairway in Rio de Janeiro to a small, funky cafe in one of Melbourne's smart suburbs. Yet Fred Ganim has managed to bridge the two worlds with his bold use of painted tiles. It was while holidaying in Brazil that Fred chanced upon the tiled steps leading to the neighbourhood of Santa Teresa, a work-in-progress by Chilean artist Jorge Selarón. The stairway features broken tiles, crystals, mirrors and porcelain in the greens, blues and yellows of Brazil's flag.

On his return to Australia, Fred immediately began painting his own tiles in the same sunshine yellows, soft blues and grassy greens, drawing on Moroccan, Spanish and Mexican influences. Not knowing what to do with them, he suggested they be used to decorate the bathroom at the cafe where he worked. The project drew an immediate response from customers, who demanded to know where they could buy the bold, cheery tiles.

From tiles, Fred translated his design ideas into framed artwork, sketching the same intricate motifs on to huge panels of paper, which he cuts out to create a stencil-like effect.

With a sharp eye for colour and design, it's no surprise to learn that Fred's mother is Rae Ganim, one of the country's leading textile designers. As a child, Fred was always encouraged to notice colour and shape in his surroundings. And travel has opened his eyes to the clever ways in which other cultures use everyday items such as paint and tiles to embellish their surroundings. "Dad (the late Anthony Ganim) always taught me that with a little extra effort you could turn the ordinary into something special." *(Contact details, page 185.)* ✹

INSPIRATIONS

{ METROPOLIS BOOKSHOP } "They have a great selection of art, graphic design and photography books. Best bookstore in town!"
(Level 3, Curtin House, 252 Swanston Street, Melbourne.)

{ SOMEDAY GALLERY } "Run by Melbourne Fashion collective PAM, this gallery exhibits new Aussie and international artists monthly."
(Level 3b, Curtin House, 252 Swanston Street, Melbourne.)

{ CHAPEL STREET BAZAAR } "It's like a huge boutique op-shop that has heaps of golden oldies." *(217-223 Chapel Street, Prahran.)*

OPPOSITE: *Fred Ganim's tile-painting career began after a holiday in Brazil.*

CAMERON COMER

{ HOME ACCESSORIES DESIGNER / STYLIST }

Couture details inspire Cameron Comer: the asymmetrical hemline of a vintage Jeanne Lanvin dress, the drape of a Balenciaga balloon skirt, the hand-bound edge of a silk neck scarf. But Cameron's is the world of couture cushions rather than clothing. After establishing the fashion label Comer and King in 1994, Cameron realised there was a gap in the market for high-quality interiors products.

Applying haute couture techniques learnt at the Paris American Academy art and fashion design school, the impeccably groomed and mannered designer started making exquisitely tailored cushions, lampshades and other home accessories. His business has evolved to the point where it offers a range of services, including interior, furniture and event design, visual merchandising and custom-made lighting. But it is cushions that most fire his interest. "They have such a simple structure, but make so much impact on a room."

A fan of the glamorous Hollywood design aesthetic of the 1930s, Cameron says his work is driven by textiles. He takes luxurious apparel fabrics – contemporary and vintage silks, linens and velvets, including remnants from famed European couture houses – and applies ideas gleaned from cocktail and evening wear. Some cushions might be embellished with embroidered or beaded details or a piece of fine French lace. Others might have an element of the unexpected – a detachable vintage brooch, perhaps, or a shocking-pink silk lining revealed only when the cushion is unzipped.

The result has the quality of a well-made garment. "We're not saving lives here." he says. "It's about luxury and delight." *(Contact and stockist details, page 183.)* ❧

INSPIRATIONS

{ DE MILLE DECORATIVE & FINE ARTS } "For beautiful and eccentric lamps and 20th century collectibles." *(7 Crossley Street, Melbourne.)*

{ MARAIS } "Gorgeous French salon interior in this wonderful fashion store." *(Level 1, Royal Arcade, 314 Little Collins Street, Melbourne.)*

{ NATIONAL GALLERY OF VICTORIA INTERNATIONAL } "One of my favourite buildings: simple and beautiful in its scale and presence." *(180 St Kilda Road, Melbourne.)*

OPPOSITE: *Cameron Comer applies haute couture techniques to soft furnishings and other home accessories.*

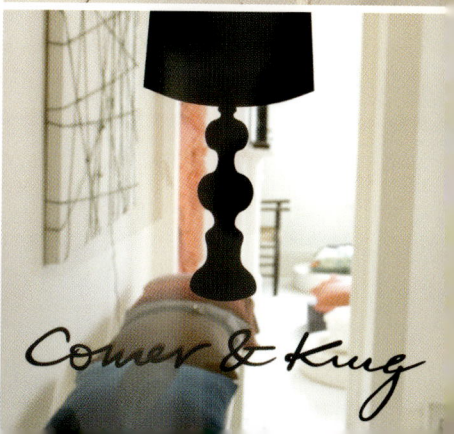

Comer & Krug

BARBARA RICHARDS
{ LAMPSHADE MAKER }

The well-worn oak floorboards of Barbara Richard's colourful workspace are littered with tufts of faux fur, fabric remnants and curls of satin ribbon. But the visitor's eye is quickly drawn to several flamboyant lampshades that evoke images of the Mad Hatter's tea party. Barbara says her lampshades are more akin to frocks than hats: "I see them as couture for lights," says the former fashion accessories buyer.

Barbara's lifelong fascination with unusual fabrics and exotic trims is evident in her work. So, too, is a sense of playfulness. It is not unusual to find tiny feathered birds perched among delicate handmade magnolia flowers, or to discover that her Le Cirque de Cravat shades have been made from vintage neckties. Her talent for tailoring ensures that each fully lined lampshade looks as good inside as out.

Having switched from accessories importer to "human pincushion", Barbara could not be more content. Despite working long hours with needle and thread she still feels "sick with excitement" when she discovers an unusual fabric or learns a new method. She thinks nothing of combining clothing rescued from opportunity shops, old girdles, furnishing fabrics, exotic silks – whatever it takes to create the look she seeks. And if she cannot find the right "bit", she improvises with paint, dye or embroidery. But mostly Barbara draws on the vast array of fabrics and trims she collected during her world travels as a fashion buyer.

Contemporary designers such as Vivienne Westwood provide inspiration, as do books on 18th and 19th century fashion, when "clothing was the status symbol and artisans took time to make truly beautiful things". Centuries later, that same spirit guides this Melbourne artisan, whose bespoke lampshades sell for $400 upwards. *(Contact and stockist details, page 189.)* 🌸

INSPIRATIONS

{ KAZARI WAREHOUSE } "I'm always trawling through mountains of fabric looking for the one that talks to me." *(7-11 Hill Street, Richmond.)*

{ BUNNINGS WAREHOUSE } "Hilarious, isn't it, but true. I start at one corner and walk up and down every aisle, drawing inspiration from all sorts of nonsense." *(3 Nepean Highway, Mentone, and other locations.)*

{ ARTISAN BOOKS } "What I do is all about history. I can open a book on flute-making and get ideas." *(159 Gertrude Street, Fitzroy.)*

OPPOSITE: *For her lamps, Barbara Richards draws on a collection of fabrics and trims she accumulated during her world travels as a fashion buyer.*

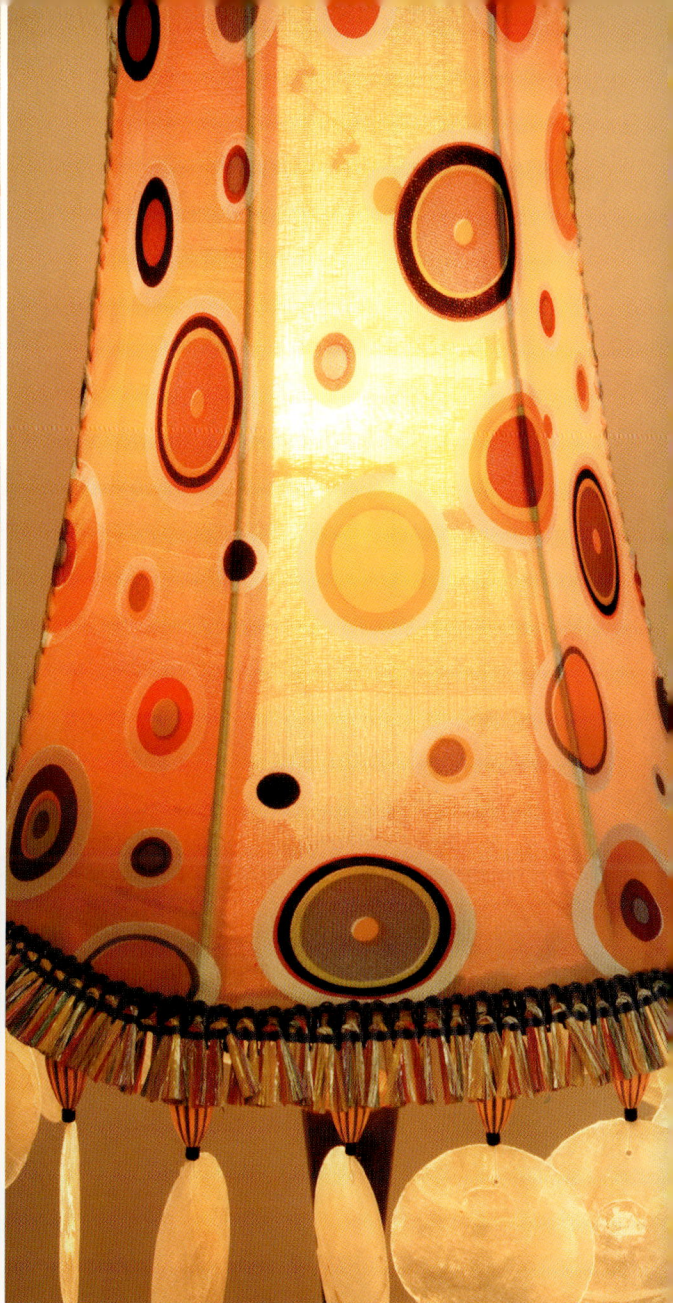

CHRIS PLUMRIDGE

{ CERAMICIST }

Chris Plumridge studied art and design at college but it was not until he was diagnosed with a potentially life-threatening illness that he immersed himself in ceramics. With a newfound sense of urgency, he bought an industrial-sized kiln, intending to make large hand-built vessels, but quickly switched focus to functional tableware when he discovered how difficult and costly such large objects were to produce. More than 20 years on, the "sense of inevitable departure" has lifted, thanks to advances in drug treatments, and Chris is still deriving immense satisfaction from making tea cups, teapots, bowls, vases and platters, under the Claystone Pottery label.

Working from a large, well-lit factory in Melbourne's south, Chris employs a traditional slip-casting method, which involves pouring liquid porcelain into moulds, and kiln-firing them. Once glazed, the pieces are fired for a second time. Slip-casting allows Chris to explore gently distorted shapes and brings a certain lightness to his work that can be difficult to achieve using a hand-thrown technique. "I like the fact that my vessels can be consistently repeated – that I can make a set of three or four things." He also enjoys experimenting with different glazes: a penchant for gelato colours and muted greens is evident throughout the factory.

The former ceramics teacher says his work is as meaningful to him today as it was 20 years ago. Beautiful tableware, he believes, can "remind us of our responsibility to nourish ourselves with healthy ingredients and aesthetics". *(Contact and stockist details, page 189.)* ✹

INSPIRATIONS

{ CRAFT VICTORIA } "You will discover many exotic handmade creations here." *(31 Flinders Lane, Melbourne.)*

{ WILKINS AND KENT } "Where furniture and artisan creativity are showcased." *(230 Brunswick Street, Fitzroy; see also page 86.)*

{ T2 } "This is a place where fine handcrafted and mass-produced teawares sit well together – a delightful surprise." *(340 Brunswick Street, Fitzroy, and other locations. Full details, page 191.)*

OPPOSITE: *Ceramicist Chris Plumridge believes beautiful tableware 'reminds us of our responsibility to nourish ourselves.'.*

WENDY GOLDEN

{ BASKET MAKER }

Wendy Golden's interest in craft germinated in her parents' sprawling country garden. She recalls afternoons spent helping her grandmother gather flowers and twigs for floral arrangements and watching birds build nests. But it was not until four decades later, while an aged-care activities coordinator, that Wendy attended a handcraft training course and made her first cane basket. In doing so, she discovered her creative calling.

Now one of Australia's foremost fibre artists, amid a worldwide resurgence of interest in basketry, this down-to-earth craftswoman works with myriad materials, including fishing line, cardboard, willow, bush litter and garden refuse. Recent works have included platters and life-size human forms woven from brightly coloured plasticised cane.

Having studied various cultures' weaving techniques, including those of Australian Aborigines and South African communities who work with telephone wire, she enjoys exploring different woven forms. "The material often dictates what I'm going to do with it," says Wendy, whose only tools are her hands and a good pair of scissors. The finer the material, the longer it may take to weave. Some pieces are completed in an afternoon; others take more than 80 hours.

Formerly working from home, Wendy was one of the first Melbourne artisans to take up residency in the newly renovated Abbotsford Convent in 2005. Although only a few kilometres from the city, the view of gum trees and bush from her window gives her the illusion of being back in the country and provides a constant reminder of her grandmother's early influence. *(Contact and stockist details, page 185.)* ✿

INSPIRATIONS

{ CRAFT VICTORIA } "A wide range of beautifully handmade products." *(31 Flinders Lane, Melbourne.)*

{ REVERSE ART TRUCK } "Supplier of manufactured detritus that can inspire an entirely new product." *(17 Greenwood Avenue, Ringwood.)*

{ McCLELLAND GALLERY AND SCULPTURE PARK } "Inspiring sculpture exhibits." *(390 McClelland Drive, Langwarrin.)*

OPPOSITE: *Wendy Golden is one of Australia's foremost fibre artists.*

MARC PASCAL

{ LIGHTING AND CERAMICS DESIGNER }

He might be a mid-career designer but there is something eternally childlike about Marc Pascal. After more than two decades' study and work in art-related fields, he remains as fascinated as ever by colour and form. "My colour palette is always evolving," enthuses Marc, who is perhaps best known for eye-catching lights made from hand-dyed polycarbonate. "I could be dyeing all my life and still come up with wonderful, different nuances."

While some components used in Marc's lights are made by outside manufacturers, the assembly and plastics dyeing is done by hand. Darting from one work-in-progress to another across the industrial warehouse he shares with four part-time assistants and a close-knit group of artists, Marc explains how each lamp is assembled. His delicate Eyoi Yoi lamp – a modern take on the chandelier – features some 90 translucent polycarbonate shapes that must be dyed and suspended from stainless steel wires. His signature corset-shaped Worvo lamp – now in its 11th year of production and often featured in top interior design magazines – is equally complex in its construction, the weaving alone taking about two hours to complete. Each lamp is made, and often coloured, to order. Also known for his organic-shaped ceramic vases that are slip-cast then hand-finished, Marc is first and foremost a designer who works across any medium that takes his fancy. "I aim to empower a space with objects that are both sensual and functional." *(Contact details, page 188.)* ❧

INSPIRATIONS

{ CRAFT VICTORIA } "I love their shows and find the different media very stimulating." *(31 Flinders Lane, Melbourne.)*

{ SPACE FURNITURE } "Good for a browse to see what's up." *(629 Church Street, Richmond.)*

{ ART STRETCHERS } "Love the smell of the place – the linen, paper and paint." *(76 Victoria Street, Carlton.)*

OPPOSITE: *Marc Pascal's lighting designs include the Eyoi Yoi table lamp (bottom right).* **THIS PAGE:** *His signature Worvo lamp.*

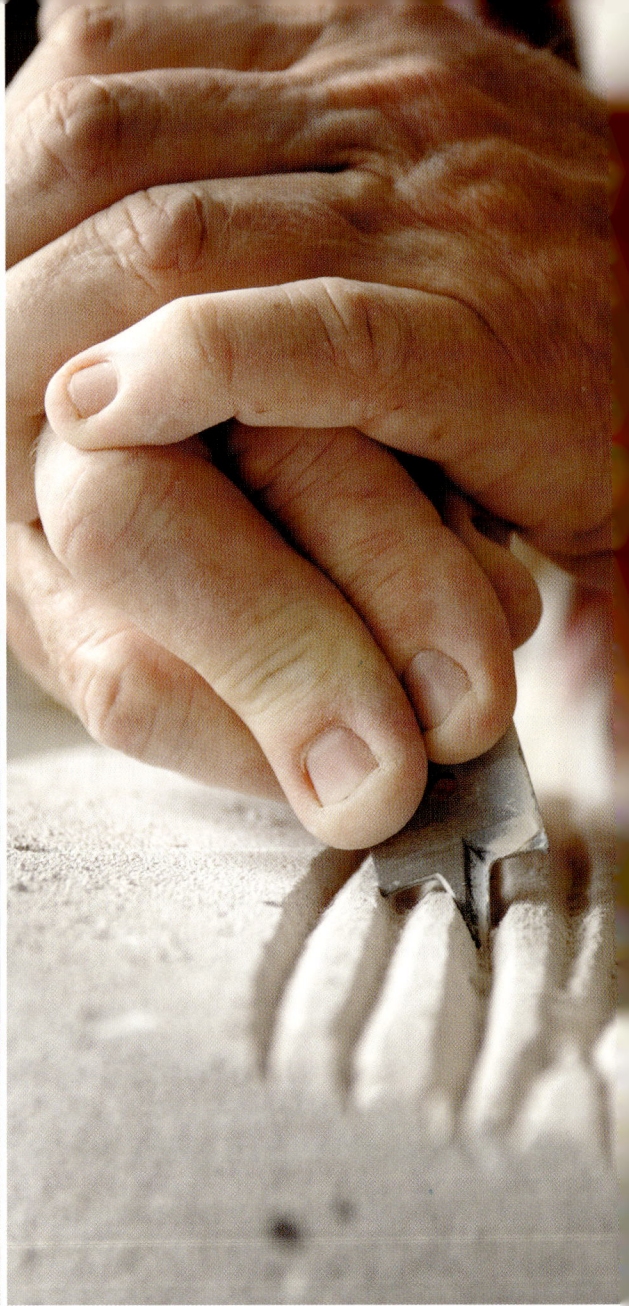

PETER McLISKY

{ STONE CARVER }

Peter McLisky almost disappears in a cloud of alabaster-white powder as he smoothes the sensuous curves of one of his works with fine sandpaper. Dust is omnipresent in Peter's working day but the former graphic designer clearly relishes the challenge of transforming a lifeless block of concrete into sculpture that might celebrate curves or planes.

Like many modern-day artisans, Peter turned a weekend hobby – carving stone sculpture on his inner-city balcony – into a business after being retrenched. Recognising a gap in the market for affordable garden sculpture and water features, he experimented with several sculpting media before settling on aerated concrete – a building product known commercially as Hebel. Unlike much natural stone, Hebel is relatively inexpensive, light and easily carved.

Peter believes his skill as a craftsman lies in ensuring that his work with this potentially sterile medium never looks "too finished". An eclectic array of tools, among them a garden pruning saw and a farrier's file, helps him achieve a less-than-perfect finish, so that the result is more reminiscent of carved natural stone. Working with an assistant, Stefan Meyers, a fine arts graduate specialising in sculpture, each piece takes between two and 10 hours to complete.

The New Zealand-born designer attended art school during the 1960s and still finds that the period influences his work. Simple graphic shapes – circles, triangles and squares – appear in many of his designs. He also draws inspiration from found objects such as pebbles, shells, seed pods, and Aboriginal and Pacific art.

To add colour to his work – which is sold through garden stores and on commission to architects and designers – Peter sometimes applies metal finishes or gold leaf. Left untreated, the water features weather to the texture of sandstone. *(Contact details, page 187.)* 🦋

INSPIRATIONS

{ CRAFT VICTORIA } "A fabulous array of well-made pieces." *(31 Flinders Lane, Melbourne.)*

{ SPACE FURNITURE } "Good examples of well-designed and crafted contemporary furniture." *(629 Church Street, Richmond.)*

{ NGV SHOP } "An excellent source of reference material." *(NGV Australia, corner Russell and Flinders Streets, Melbourne, and NGV International, 180 St Kilda Road, Melbourne.)*

OPPOSITE: *Peter McLisky works with an array of tools to achieve a 'less-than-perfect' finish.*

GREG HATTON

{ FURNITURE MAKER }

A former fisheries and wildlife officer, Greg Hatton saw firsthand the destruction caused by willow trees. Originally introduced to stabilise cleared riverbanks, the trees choke smaller waterways, leading to flooding and bank erosion. But when Greg visits degraded riverbeds around Victoria today, he views the environmental pest with new eyes. Using simple hand tools – secateurs or a bow saw – he harvests the coppice growth from around the base and paints the cuts with herbicide to prevent further growth, leaving the trunk intact to ensure the riverbank remains stable. Then, he fashions the willow canes into rustic tables, chairs and garden accessories.

The part-time garden landscaper has long had an interest in woodwork; he built a cubby when he was a child and, with a "waste not, want not" attitude, has made furniture from scrounged offcuts for years. It was while researching willow control on the internet that he discovered the European tradition of making furniture from the trees.

Following centuries-old techniques, Greg conditions and bends the canes into shape across his knee. A standard chair takes about a day to make, from harvest to final nail. Greg enjoys adding a twist to traditional European and American bent willow furniture styles. A contrived imbalance – a determinedly crooked cane placed across the back of an armchair, contorted timbers bracing a coffee table – gives his creations a sculptural quality that suits both traditional and contemporary settings. He eschews varnish and other painted finishes, preferring to let the willow weather naturally. Prices range from $250 for a stool to $800 for a two-seater bench. Greg also makes gates from unsawn timber.

If the weather is fine, the fit and perennially tanned furniture maker sometimes begins construction in the shade of the willows. But mostly he works in his sheltered backyard, a block from St Kilda beach. "Working with raw materials and simple tools opens a window to a life lived simply and practically." *(Contact and stockist details, page 185.)* ✿

INSPIRATIONS

{ HUDSON CLOTHES } "Their quirky accessories made in small runs – belts, scarves and badges – are great for presents." *(229 Carlisle Street, Balaclava.)*

{ BEAUFORT'S BIG GARAGE SALE } "An eclectic mix of bits and pieces – he's my source of rusty bolts." *(31 Neill Street, Beaufort, near Ballarat.)*

{ VEG OUT COMMUNITY GARDENS ST KILDA } "Being community-based, these gardens are made up of many different people's efforts but they all blend together beautifully." *(Corner Shakespeare Grove and Chaucer Street, St Kilda.)*

OPPOSITE: *Greg Hatton uses techniques that are centuries old to fashion his rustic furniture.*

SIMON LLOYD
{ PRODUCT DESIGNER }

Simon Lloyd has been intrigued since he was a child by the way things are put together. Aged six, he attempted to build a model boat from balsa wood and papier-mâché. The almost two-metre model eventually collapsed under the weight of paper and paste, but the exercise left Simon with a clearer understanding of materials' strength.

Decades on, he is still playing around with different materials. Best known for his felt and ceramic work, the British-born designer also uses a wide palette of materials, including cast iron, plywood and steel, to create functional objects such as lights, trays and bowls. Although trained in furniture design, Simon prefers to make small objects that can be "held and cradled" and, importantly, are made to last – his label, Sisu, is the Finnish word for endurance.

The piece that cemented his career was an organic-shaped ceramic vase, first produced in 1995 and sold through high-end retailers in London, Paris, Copenhagen and Australia. More recently, he has earned international recognition for his simple felt dishes. Inspired by Aboriginal bark gathering bowls, Simon's dishes feature unusual hand-stitched joints that alleviate the need for a corner seam. His mind overflows with ideas, and producing one thing inevitably leads to the next. His experimentation with chipped ceramics, for example, resulted in the development of a high-tech ceramic knife. Inspired by Japanese contemporary architecture, childhood memories and contemporary jazz, Simon works across projects and on demand. One day he might be found sitting at his kitchen table, tinkering with a prototype cast-iron pan, the next might be spent in his studio preparing clay models for slip-casting.

Simplicity is his guiding principle. "The level of complexity is far too high these days. I want people to be able to look at what I've made and understand how it was made." *(Contact details, page 187.)* ✳

INSPIRATIONS

{ THE MERCHANT OF FAIRNESS } "This second-hand book store is a wonderful source of architectural, design and trade books." *(300 Whitehorse Road, Balwyn, and store 138, South Melbourne Market, York Street, South Melbourne.)*

{ BOY AND GIRL TOY SHOP } "Beautiful early Bauhaus wooden blocks and puzzles with a strong design emphasis." *(495 High Street, Prahran.)*

{ INDUSTRIA } "Functional objects that shine." *(202 Gertrude Street, Fitzroy.)*

OPPOSITE: *Simon Lloyd prefers to make small objects that can be held and cradled, including his felt dishes (far right and top).*

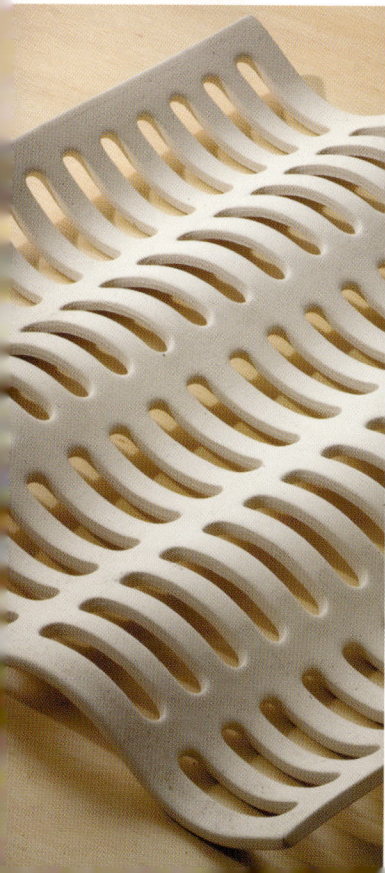

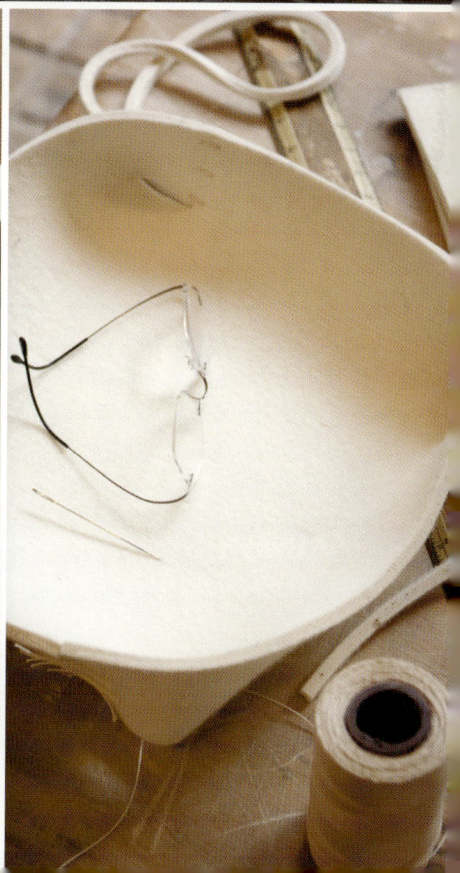

ANNA LORENZETTO
{ LEATHER HOMEWARES DESIGNER }

Anna Lorenzetto is fastidious and it shows. It shows in the way she has meticulously grouped glass vases and ornaments, sourced from op-shops, on a sideboard in her studio. It shows in the way the orange lining of her vintage black coat teams perfectly with the polka-dotted orange scarf looped artfully about her neck. But mostly it shows in her leatherwork – in the tightly stitched edges of a floor pad, the smooth finish on a bookend and in the perfect rounded "belly" of a cylindrical clothes hamper. "I put a lot of thought into detail," Anna says. The thickness of the cotton thread, the length of the stitch and the distance of the seam from the edge all come in for close scrutiny. "The finish of the product is everything."

Graduating in 1997 with an honours degree in industrial design, Anna set out to create her own luxurious leather homewares. Searching for a master leather craftsperson to bring her designs to life, Anna was introduced to Carlo Visentin, who had extensive experience making prestige leather accessories. Both of Italian descent, the designer and leatherworker share a close working relationship. Anna credits Carlo's finesse for much of her success. "I would never have been able to push the material to its limits," she says. "Carlo taught me everything I know about leather."

Anna's designs, crafted from fine New Zealand hides hand-finished and dyed to her specifications in strong autumnal colours, blacks and modernist white, beg to be touched, caressed, even smelt. "I couldn't do anything that wasn't in some way sensual," says Anna, gliding her French-manicured fingers along a perfectly stitched leather seam.
(Contact and stockist details, page 187.) 🌺

INSPIRATIONS

{ JOB WAREHOUSE FABRIC SALES } "My mum first took me there as a kid. I particularly love searching for old fabrics." *(56 Bourke Street, Melbourne.)*

{ ZOMP SHOEZ } "They have great shoes. I buy, but sometimes I just go to look at the treatment of the leather – how it is manipulated." *(271 Little Collins Street, Melbourne, and shop 9, 546 Chapel Street, South Yarra.)*

{ NSW LEATHER CO } "Great job-lots of leather. Amazing colours and special finishes. If I want to make a special gift for someone, I know I can come here and find leather that is out of the ordinary." *(107-109 Sackville Street, Collingwood.)*

OPPOSITE: *Anna Lorenzetto (top left) and Carlo Visentin.*

VICKI MURFETT

Vicki Murfett's world view is like no other's. When she looks at a lamp base, she doesn't see a light source. She sees a potential foundation for swirls of tiny pale pink limpet, cockle or even scallop shells. Gazing at chandeliers, vases, mirrors and picture frames draws the same response. In fact, if Vicki had her way, every wall and ceiling of her tiny home studio would be embellished with smooth, curvaceous shells. "That might be a little dramatic," she admits. "Perhaps I'll shell large boards instead and place them against the walls."

The idea is not without precedent: Vicki draws much inspiration from the gallery at A La Ronde house in Devon, England, which was encrusted with millions of shells by its eccentric spinster owners in 1795. Vicki became enamored of shells after being given a collection by a friend's mother in 1991. "I found them so incredibly beautiful, all their wonderful shapes, forms and colours." Although involved with decoupage at the time, she immediately switched crafts, and starting decorating small boxes and hand-held mirrors with shells.

Her first private commission was for a birthday party in 1994, when she was asked to decorate giant candelabras for the historic cellars at Seppelt Great Western Winery in western Victoria.

Former Georges buyer Christine Barro saw some of her work and encouraged Vicki to sell her pieces at the now-defunct department store. Today, Vicki scours auction houses and antique markets for mirrors, picture frames and candlesticks that she can embellish with shells and coral, which she sources mainly from Queensland. "Whenever I see a piece of furniture, I immediately visualise it covered in shells." *(Contact and stockist details, page 188.)* 🦐

INSPIRATIONS

{ CHRISTINE } Accessories maven Christine Barro combs the world for delectable bags, scarves, belts and jewellery for her subterranean boutique. *(181 Flinders Lane, Melbourne.)*

{ NATIONAL GALLERY OF VICTORIA INTERNATIONAL } "I love this place – I find it so inspirational." *(180 St Kilda Road, Melbourne.)*

{ WESTERN PORT COASTLINE FROM FLINDERS TO SOMERS } "Great for collecting shells, rope, feathers and driftwood."

OPPOSITE: *Vicki Murfett switched from decoupage to working with shells.*

KRIS COAD

{ CERAMICIST }

Most people who encounter Kris Coad's hand-thrown ceramics for the first time feel compelled to touch them. There is something strangely seductive about the ripples that characterise her tableware. In contrast to the way most potters work, Kris prefers to retain the "throwing lines" (ridges) that form as the clay spins on the pottery wheel, so that when someone holds one of her cups or bowls, they feel the imprint of her hand.

Completing a Master's in Fine Arts in 2002, Kris explored various clay types, eventually settling on porcelain for her tableware, which looks delicate but is surprisingly durable. Positioned at her wheel before a window that looks out to gum trees and native shrubbery at Albert Park's Gasworks Arts Park, Kris works for hours on end, sometimes six days a week. She enjoys making functional items that add pleasure to the ritual of eating and drinking. Some of her tableware – notably sake cups, olive oil dispensers and dumpling trays – result from collaborations with chefs and food retailers, including Kris's good friend Misuzu Kawano, of the Albert Park restaurant Misuzu's. Most of her designs however, are based on her drawings.

Translucency is a recurring theme in Kris's work. Holding a salad bowl to the light, she enthuses about how it is possible to see the shadows cast by leaves through the vessel. "That sort of thing fascinates me," she says. "It's about a play of light and about knowing what is inside."

For exhibition pieces, Kris slip-casts fine bone china to create delicate reliefs based on Christian and Buddhist iconography, such as the mandorla (overlapping circles that form an almond shape). A recent work – a suspended canopy of bone china leaves – uses light to generate internal markings, patterning and shadows. Sipping tea from one of Kris's beakers, it is no surprise to learn that she has never forgotten the words of ceramics lecturer Shunichi Inoue: "Any vessel touching your lips must kiss your lips." *(Contact and stockist details, page 183.)*

INSPIRATIONS

{ ROYAL BOTANIC GARDENS MELBOURNE } "I hold these gardens dear to my heart. I often go there to work through an idea." *(Birdwood Avenue, South Yarra.)*

{ SOUTH MELBOURNE FORESHORE } "I love that you can see the horizon. There is no clutter in your vision – you just look out to the sea."

{ CITY OF PORT PHILLIP LIBRARIES } "I'm an avid reader and these libraries are a great resource." *(Corner Montague Street and Dundas Place, Albert Park, and other locations.)*

OPPOSITE: *When someone holds a Kris Coad cup or bowl, they will feel the imprint of the artist's hands.*

MARK MARINATO
{ MIRROR MAKER }

At first glance, the frames of Mark Marinato's imposing mirrors look like antiques made from heavy oxidised metal. It comes as a surprise to learn that he has made them almost entirely of timber, embellished, perhaps, with old Chinese coins or upholstery tacks. Mark's elaborate detailing gives these mirrors their individuality. Customers often comment that they find it hard to tell whether the mirrors are framed in metal, leather or ceramic.

Mark stumbled into his craft. In the early '90s, he offered to make mirrors to brighten the entrances of two apartments that a property developer friend was selling. The prospective buyers were so enamoured of the mirrors that they wouldn't buy the properties without them. Commissions from restaurateurs and interior designers gradually followed.

Each frame starts as flat sections of timber into which Mark carves ornamental notches and grooves. He then gradually builds up the finish by painting, sanding and repainting the frame with up to 10 coats to achieve the appearance of a time-worn patina. Along the way, he adds decorative details – a corbel unearthed at a junk shop, stamps from an old leather factory or coins found at a Bali market. And the finishing touch? Belgian glass mirrors – the best available, according to Mark. Depending on its size, a frame could take up to three weeks to make. An imposing mirror three metres by two metres might sell for around $2500.

"I wanted to take mirrors to another level whereby the frame would be likened to a canvas that could be personalised to suit any client or decor need, but maintain an integrity and craft that embodied an artisan's appreciation," he says. *(Contact and stockist details, page 187.)* ✳

INSPIRATIONS

{ DOMAIN FLOWERS } "They have the most imaginative floral installations as part of their changing window displays. I've seen nothing like their creative, offbeat approach." *(183 Domain Road, South Yarra.)*

{ LIBBY EDWARDS GALLERIES } "Seldom has there been anything on show here that isn't completely stimulating to view." *(1046 High Street, Armadale.)*

{ ST KILDA ESPLANADE ARTS & CRAFT MARKET }
"Not only to source oddments for my frames, but to view the wide spectrum of art dynamics." *(Sundays, Upper Esplanade, St Kilda.)*

OPPOSITE: *Mark Marinato's mirror frames receive up to 10 coats of paint.*

ANNA CHARLESWORTH

{ METAL ARTIST }

It is no overstatement to describe some of Anna Charlesworth's work as majestic. Her wrought-iron doors often soar to heights of more than three metres, transforming an otherwise ordinary entrance into something spectacular. "A door is like an exclamation mark. It can make sense of a home," says the softly spoken metal artist, whose body of work also includes shelves, lights, balustrades and tables.

Having travelled around Spain in the 1980s after completing an arts degree in Melbourne, Anna finds she is still inspired by the Spanish design sensibility – from the sinuous architecture of Antoni Gaudí to the bold abstract expressionist paintings of Antoni Tàpies. Leaves and scrolls, cut by hand or laser, lend an Art Nouveau feel to some of her pieces, but all have a strong contemporary edge.

Returning to Melbourne in the late 1980s, Anna was drawn to the flamboyant work of glass and metal artist Mark Douglass. Her youthful enthusiasm persuaded the more experienced metalworker to offer her an apprenticeship, even though she had never picked up a power tool. Five years later, she ventured out on her own and now works on commission alongside fellow metalworker Neal Millard, whose extensive welding experience she frequently draws upon.

Surrounded by scrap metal yards and seemingly deserted warehouses in Melbourne's inner west, Anna and Neal's studio evokes the image of a rustic farm shed. Welding, grinding and forging are punishing tasks but Anna finds the work meditative. "The actual process of making something is the best part of my working day. The minute you start working on the materials you see it start to come together like a large jigsaw puzzle." *(Contact details, page 183.)* 🗡

INSPIRATIONS

{ E.G.ETAL } "Gorgeous and unusual pieces of jewellery – something for everyone." *(185 Little Collins Street and 167 Flinders Lane, Melbourne.)*

{ OTTOMAN CLASSICS } "Inspiring ceramics from Turkey and Syria." *(155 Sydney Road, Brunswick.)*

{ THE TRAVELLERS SCULPTURE } "Beautiful public art that tells a story. An ingenious feat of engineering." *(Sandridge Bridge, Melbourne.)*

OPPOSITE: *Spanish design has influenced the work of metal artist Anna Charlesworth.*

BERN EMMERICHS

{ CERAMICIST }

When Bern Emmerichs was a Melbourne art student in the early 1980s, she never imagined that her work would find its way into the homes of international celebrities such as Janet Jackson, Björk and Rachel Griffiths. Yet two decades later, the market for her hand-painted and highly personalised ceramic pieces spans the globe.

It was a trip to Spain and Italy after college that ignited Bern's interest in painted ceramics. Back in Melbourne, she "went ballistic", covering the floors and walls of her home with hand-painted tiles. Experimentation with mosaics followed. But it is her whimsical hand-painted platters for which Bern is best known. Often commissioned as wedding presents or one-off gifts, the platters are personalised with intricate illustrations, transfers, snippets of information and even secrets that she gleans by interviewing her clients. She also hand-paints tiles, which might be used to create a mural, a splashback, a table or a feature on a fireplace. Another interesting recent commission involved decorating a hand-crafted surfboard for musician Ben Harper.

She works from her rustic renovated home in Windsor, which she shares with her two daughters and German-born husband Gerhard, a master glass painter who also works with metal and wood. In every room, their work and that of other artists jostles for space with flea-market finds and treasured antiques. Out the back, the couple's purpose-built "his and hers" studios overlook a lush garden featuring an enchanting juxtaposition of olive trees, palms, lipstick-pink impatiens and trailing vines. Between the studios is a small hut housing an industrial-sized kiln.

A love of poetry, history and horses gives Bern inspiration, whether for commissioned works or for self-expression. Her creative husband is another key influence. Above all, her vibrant work comes from the heart. It is, says Bern, "a romantic celebration of life and its gifts".
(Bern Emmerichs, 13 Hornby Street, Windsor. Full details, page 184.)

INSPIRATIONS

{ REVERSE ART TRUCK } A warehouse full of factory and industry discards and offcuts – "odds and ends that set off one's creative juices".
(17 Greenwood Avenue, Ringwood.)

{ CAMBERWELL SUNDAY MARKET } "Great for the unpredictable array of old books and curios." *(Station Street, Camberwell.)*

{ RED STITCH ACTORS THEATRE } "Always a fresh inspiration involving brilliant acting in a cosy and intimate setting." *(Rear 2 Chapel Street, St Kilda.)*

OPPOSITE: *Bern Emmerich's hand-painted ceramics are personalised, often with snippets of secret information she gleans by interviewing clients.*

ANDREW WOOD

{ WOOD WORKER }

Andrew Wood's love affair with Australian timber is evident wherever you look in his sprawling Edwardian home. His sought-after wooden sculptures – designed to twist and bend towards the sunlight – make an intriguing statement in the family living room, while his dining room-cum-storeroom is packed with precious pieces of raw timber awaiting their maker's attention. Outside, red gum fence posts lie soaking in a tub of water to keep them from drying out before use.

A former environmental landscaper with a background in architecture, Andrew shifted to woodworking in 2000, in what he views as a natural progression. "A table is very much like a building, only the viewing angle has changed," he says. Initially, he made contemporary timber furniture but more recently he has begun experimenting with homewares and sculptural pieces crafted from green wood – freshly cut timber with a high water content.

His latest works, made on commission, celebrate the fact that wood moves with changes in the external environment. Now, rather than worrying about drawers sticking or tabletops warping, he rejoices when a client phones to say that something he made has twisted. His trays curve gently, the result of steam being applied to the wood before assembly. The sensuous, rippled patina makes stroking them irresistible. Screens, made from slender red gum rods anchored at one end to a wooden block, also explore the concept of moving wood. "The rods are green when cut. As they dry they will continue to twist and bend, revealing hidden stresses that lie within the wood."

Andrew works with about 10 Australian timbers, sourced from local suppliers who specialise in recycled timber and environmentally friendly practices. As he sees it, working with Australian timbers helps him relate to the land. "Timber grains reveal all sorts of interesting traces of that tree's history – fine insect calligraphy, drought, fire and distress. By working with green wood, the stories hidden within the fibres are revealed through movement and texture."
(Contact and stockist details, page 191.) ✿

INSPIRATIONS

{ BOWERBIRD SAVED TIMBERS } "At last, a timber supplier who is sympathetic to the artist and prepared to help me select the wood." *(Old Millgrove Sawmill, 3045 Warburton Highway, Millgrove, Upper Yarra Valley.)*

{ INNER CITY GARDEN SUPPLIES } "This is the only place that I know of that has quality green red gum in the form of fence posts." *(6 Kirkdale Street, Brunswick East.)*

OPPOSITE: *Andrew Wood's pieces celebrate movement and texture.*

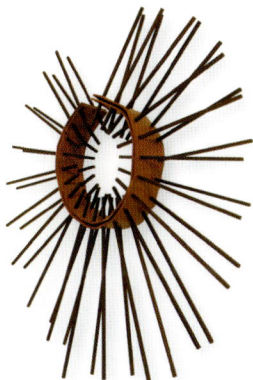

PHILIP STOKES

{ GLASS ARTIST }

Four people stand before a raging furnace, each awaiting their cue. At a nearby bench, blowpipes, tong-like tweezers, jacks and wooden paddles lie in readiness. When Philip Stokes extracts a lava-like blob of molten glass from the furnace, the team springs into action, working with the precision of surgeons and the flair of circus entertainers. Over the next three hours they twist and turn the glass, layer it with colour, return it to the furnace, extract it again, and roll and shape it. Finally, a work of art emerges, in this case, a glistening hollow sculpture that recalls a bird in flight, part of a 22-piece glass installation that will be suspended in the lobby of Hong Kong's Four Seasons Hotel.

It was the theatre of glass-blowing that initially attracted Philip to the craft. Having worked for several years as an actor and director after graduating from drama school, Philip found handling hot glass surprisingly similar. "Like the theatre, spontaneity, improvisation and chance are all key elements in crafting glass," he says. Philip's work, which ranges from large glass sculptures to small production pieces such as clean-lined bowls and vases, is inspired by organic forms and Scandinavian design. Another key influence is Philip's mother, Helen Stokes, who has won international recognition for her unusual method of casting glass.

At Abbotsford Convent, Philip has established a large workshop and gallery, where he hopes to share with visitors the excitement of glass-making. "Like nothing else, glass captures the light and the imagination of the artisan and the viewer." (*Philip Stokes Studio Glass, Abbotsford Convent Mercator Laundry, 1 St Heliers Street, Abbotsford. Full details, page 190.*) ✸

INSPIRATIONS

{ VERONICA GEORGE GALLERY } "For her beautiful presentation of contemporary glass." *(1082 High Street, Armadale.)*

{ ABBOTSFORD CONVENT } "For its majestic grandness and insight into Melbourne's rich past." *(1 St Heliers Street, Abbotsford.)*

{ BLACK ROCK } "For the sun, sand, sea and leisure that makes Melbourne my home."

OPPOSITE: *Philip Stokes is attracted to the theatre of glass blowing.*

PLEASURE

MUSICAL INSTRUMENTS
CARDS AND JOURNALS
TOYS
FOOD

JAMES CATTELL
{ TOY MAKER / SCULPTOR }

MARIANNA DI BARTOLO
{ BISCUIT AND SWEET MAKER }

BECK WHEELER
{ ARTIST / TEXTILE SCULPTOR }

JACK POMPEI
{ BOAT BUILDER }

BENEDICT PUGLISI
{ STRINGED INSTRUMENT MAKER }

NEIL OKE
{ SURFBOARD MAKER }

JUDY CAMERON
{ TOY MAKER }

LACHLAN FISHER
{ CRICKET BAT MAKER }

ADRIENNE CHISHOLM
{ PUPPET MAKER / DESIGNER }

IAN WATCHORN
{ STRINGED INSTRUMENT MAKER }

ALANA WATERSON
& SARA DICKINS
{ STATIONERY DESIGNERS }

LEON PETROFF
{ VIOLIN MAKER }

DANIEL CHIRICO
{ BAKER }

GRACIA HABY
& LOUISE JENNISON
{ JOURNAL MAKERS / ARTISTS }

CAROLYN IMLACH
{ SOAP MAKER }

ARNO BACKES
{ CHOCOLATIER }

JACK SPIRA
{ GUITAR MAKER }

JANE WIFFEN
{ CUPCAKE MAKER }

ANITA MIKEDIS
{ BOTANICAL HOMEWARES DESIGNER }

JOANNE SCHOOF
{ CANDLE MAKER }

PETER LANCASTER
{ LITHOGRAPHER }

DAVID COLES
{ PAINT MAKER }

EMMA COWAN
{ CARD DESIGNER }

IRWIN AND McLAREN
BOOKBINDERS
{ BOOKBINDERS }

JOANNE SAUNDERS
{ RECORDER MAKER }

VEGETABLE SOAP

ORGANIC

JAMES CATTELL

{ TOY MAKER / SCULPTOR }

Visiting James Cattell's world is like stepping into a gothic fairytale. A gnarled wisteria vine, every bit as vigorous as Jack's beanstalk, almost smothers his timber shack studio. Inside, the visitor is confronted by bizarre odds and ends, which James fondly describes as "unfinished thoughts". Scrap metal and skeletal remains sit alongside bike gears and flotsam and jetsam from the beach, forming the basis of James's automata, or self-operating mechanical sculptures.

Working from this studio behind Honeyweather & Speight, the St Kilda toy shop he and his partner, Dorelle Davidson, opened in 1988, James also makes puppets and larger sculptures on commission. The soulful faces of his egg characters – automata with hand-painted ceramic heads – are especially poignant. Each creation exalts in a colourful name, among them Countess Wilhelmina, Consuela Maria de l'Oeuf, and the Grand Duke of Quiche. "There is something terribly sad about their desperate attempts to become human," muses James, also the author and illustrator of three children's books featuring some of his automata.

A self-taught metal-worker with a background in sculpture and puppetry, James draws inspiration from medieval history, anatomy and opera. His grandparents were another key influence. "Both sets of grandparents had fascinating old books and pieces of china, as well as stories that made history live for me."

James finds "warmth and relief" in working with his hands and creating things that are mechanical rather than electronic. He is fascinated by the idea of humanising machines and the history of automata, notably in 18th and 19th century France, when craftsmen created "toys" that could write, draw pictures and even play musical instruments. "Some of these pieces took many years to build. They were then toured as exhibition or carnival pieces to generate income." His own creations take "more time than I dare think about" and prices range from several hundred dollars to over $1000. *(Honeyweather & Speight, 113 Barkly Street, St Kilda. Full details, page 183.)* ✹

INSPIRATIONS

{ NATIONAL GALLERY OF VICTORIA INTERNATIONAL } "Especially the decorative arts section for the fascinating history of domestic objects." *(180 St Kilda Road, Melbourne.)*

{ ST KILDA SALVATION ARMY FAMILY STORE } "A great source of metal receptacles and other objects." *(90 Inkerman Street, St Kilda.)*

{ HIGHETT METAL } "For scrap metal." *(283-295 Boundary Road, Braeside.)*

OPPOSITE: *James Cattell is also the author of three children's books.*

MARIANNA DI BARTOLO

{ BISCUIT AND SWEET MAKER }

Marianna Di Bartolo has vivid childhood memories of her Sicilian relatives crowding out the family kitchen as they prepared tray upon tray of traditional biscuits for Easter and Christmas celebrations. Completing her cooking apprenticeship in 1992, Marianna honed her pastry and sweet-making skills at the acclaimed Laurent Bakery. Aged 25 and needing a break from a gruelling schedule of six-day weeks, she set off on a year-long holiday overseas, visiting relatives in Sicily on her way home. It was during this 1995 stopover that Marianna came to fully appreciate the delights of Sicilian sweets – "no Sicilian would serve coffee without them" – and began dreaming of producing them under her own label.

Back in Melbourne, she worked for several other food businesses before launching her Dolcetti ("little sweet things") label in 2005. Searching for a kitchen to lease, she happened upon a Brunswick cafe with an old but still-functional almond crusher in the back room. "The minute I saw that machine, I knew I had found my new home," she says. Freshly crushed almonds are a key component of Marianna's Sicilian nougat, cakes and biscuits, which are handmade to treasured family recipes that she has adapted to her own palate. Seasonal fruits make their way into such treats as mandarin almond biscuits and lemon polenta shortbread. She also makes preserves such as candied citrus, used in nougat. Marianna makes several kinds, including classic vanilla, honey and almond nougat and rose petal and pistachio coated in white chocolate.

Rapid expansion means Marianna now employs four part-time staff, including her mother, Lidia, to help with cake-making, packing and deliveries. Marianna attributes both her passion for cooking and her success as a chef to her mother. "Everything that I make today reflects my mother," she says. "I loved watching her cook when I was a child. What she did in the kitchen is deep within my subconscious." *(Contact and stockist details, page 184.)* ✺

INSPIRATIONS

{ MORNINGS WITH MARGARET THROSBY, ABC CLASSIC FM }
"A show that inspires me while I work away in the kitchen."

{ FARMER'S MARKET, COLLINGWOOD CHILDREN'S FARM }
"A lovely family ambience and I love seeing the seasonal products."
(Second Saturday of every month, St Heliers Street, Abbotsford.)

{ FEDERATION SQUARE } "The vision behind it, the square that brings people together and the beautiful rich and natural materials used to build it."
(Corner Swanston and Flinders Streets, Melbourne.)

OPPOSITE: *Marianna Di Bartolo attributes her success to her Sicilian mother.*

BECK WHEELER

{ ARTIST / TEXTILE SCULPTOR }

There is something unsettling about Beck Wheeler's toys. Davo the Mighty Man-Bunny, for example, is a creature with nipples, a belly button and missing teeth. He is usually seen with a can of VB beer, and lists fried chicken, dim sims and cigarettes as a few of his favourite things. He often sleeps rough because he spends his bus money on $2 peep shows and lottery tickets.

Clearly, Beck's kooky creatures come from the dark side of Toyland.

Beck, who moved from New Zealand to Melbourne in 2000 to study painting and illustration, began making her creatures four years ago in an attempt to bring to life a comic strip she was working on. When friends suggested the fabric characters would make great toys, Beck put together a small collection for an exhibition, launching her Kissy Kissy label in 2004.

Made from new and recycled fabrics, the toys resonate with children and adults alike. Fashion designer Fiona Scanlon asked for a collection for her children's wear boutique, while human-sized installations of the white vinyl Heebee Geebees have appeared in a city bar and, from wall-mounted display cases, amused pedestrians traversing the Flinders Street station underpass.

Each character begins as an illustration and is brought to life through the addition of "real" features such as breasts and nipples and an accompanying personality profile (one of Beck's Gahgoo creatures loves to bake cookies in the nude, while another wants to become a podiatrist). "I love to evoke a sense of wonder with each character by giving them a life of their own: they radiate uniqueness and embrace individuality." Beck's toys range in price from $85 for a 48-centimetre Gahgoo to $550 for a Heebee Geebee. *(Contact details, page 191.)* ✿

INSPIRATIONS

{ GEORGIELOVE.COM, ONLINE DESIGN STORE } "A great site to visit and peek at what other artists are doing and selling without having to leave the house." *(www.georgielove.com)*

{ CHAPEL STREET BAZAAR } "Quirky and left-of-centre knick-knacks." *(217-223 Chapel Street, Prahran.)*

{ OUTRÉ GALLERY } "A lot of my inspiration comes from contemporary illustration and 2D imagery. I love going into Outré, which specialises in illustration." *(249 Elizabeth Street, Melbourne.)*

OPPOSITE: *Beck Wheeler's kooky toys, including Davo (top left), come from the dark side of Toyland.*

JACK POMPEI

{ BOAT BUILDER }

If God had wanted us to sail in fibreglass boats, he would have created fibreglass trees.
At least, that's Jack Pompei's theory. The old salt, whose family has been crafting commercial
and pleasure craft in Melbourne for almost a century, believes a good boat is a timber boat.
And he likes them hewn from magnificent timbers such as mahogany, Huon pine, spotted gum,
New Zealand kauri, and celery-top pine, the golden-hued Tasmanian conifer favoured for its
strength and durability.

Jack's Italian fisherman father, Salvatore, settled in Melbourne in 1911 and established
a boatbuilding business. In time, the Pompei name became associated with exceptionally well-
built fishing trawlers, ferries, yachts, dinghies and couta boats. Jack and his brothers Joe and
John learnt boat-building from an early age and it seemed natural that they should follow their
father into the business. Jack still works from his father's original building, a hangar-like shed
on the Mordialloc foreshore surrounded by craft awaiting repair. Inside the shed, packed to the
rafters with tools and timber, blue plastic sheeting is thrown aside to reveal the rib-like interior
of a dinghy under construction. Nearby, a 60-year-old cadet dinghy made from cedar and king
billy pine is being restored and another 18-metre red gum keel awaits Jack's attention.

In a corner at the rear of the shed, dusty, faded photographs of Pompei-built boats provide
a historical timeline of the family's proud past. Jack acknowledges that there is not the demand
there once was for his painstakingly crafted timber boats. Asked to describe what he loves about
these majestic vessels, Jack doesn't miss a beat: "They feel like home." *(Pompei's of Mordialloc,
561 Main Street, Mordialloc. Full details, page 189.)*

INSPIRATIONS

{ MORDIALLOC AND THE MORDIALLOC CREEK } "This is a great suburb
with everything going for it, and it would be great to see the creek returned to the
beautiful fishing and boating spot it once was."

{ PORT PHILLIP } "It's a bay you can't trust – it's so peaceful on the right day,
but when it's angry, it's really angry."

{ RICKETTS POINT, BEAUMARIS } "It's a great spot for fishing."

OPPOSITE: *Jack and his two brothers followed their father into the
boat-building business.*

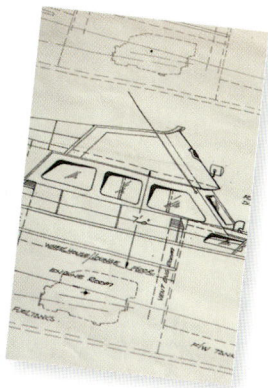

BENEDICT PUGLISI
{ STRINGED INSTRUMENT MAKER }

The smell of varnish hangs heavy in the air of Benedict Puglisi's workshop, which is cluttered with partially completed stringed instruments. Here, the techniques used to make and restore instruments have barely changed since the 17th century. Lovingly stroking a piece of European maple, Benedict recalls growing up surrounded by music in a family of music-lovers. He played bass guitar in a rock band as a teenager and became fascinated by the "physics of sound" while studying for a music degree. Eventually, he landed a job as assistant to a Melbourne-based Dutch violin-maker before starting his own business, Atelier Puglisi, in 1995.

Today, Benedict is one of Australia's leading stringed instrument makers, and Atelier Puglisi's instruments are played around the world. Customers include double bass players Régent Archambault of the Canadian folk band La Bottine Souriante and local jazz musician Vincent Wienckowski.

Of all the stringed instruments, double bass is Benedict's great love — when he listens to music, it is the bass part he hears — and he takes great care in sourcing wood to make the instruments. The bows are made from Brazilian rainforest timber, and the back and sides from maple grown in the European Alps, where the secret of choosing timber with fine acoustic properties is passed from one generation to the next.

Perfecting the varnish is critical, as it affects not only the instrument's appearance but its tone. "Recipes for varnish are like somebody's lasagne: everybody has a different one but once you find the one that works best, you stick with it." Each double bass takes up to 1000 hours to complete and can command more than $20,000. Yet even at this price, the exercise is difficult to justify financially. But for Benedict and his close-knit staff of six, the rewards are plenty – not least being able to listen to a world-renowned musician playing one of their pieces of art. *(Atelier Puglisi, 40 Church Street, Hawthorn. Full details, page 189.)* ❧

INSPIRATIONS

{ PORT PHILLIP } "For fishing, enjoying the solitude and watching the boats come in and out of Station Pier."

{ BENNETTS LANE JAZZ CLUB } "For some of the best live local jazz music Melbourne has to offer." *(25 Bennetts Lane, Melbourne.)*

{ HAMER HALL, THE ARTS CENTRE } "Inspirational for its world-class performances and a great meeting place." *(100 St Kilda Road, Melbourne.)*

OPPOSITE: *Benedict Puglisi became fascinated by the physics of sound while studying for a music degree.*

NEIL OKE

{ SURFBOARD MAKER }

With his thick tousled hair, loose-fitting jeans and thongs, Neil Oke looks every bit the beatnik surfboard maker. It's a part he has played with gusto since he was 20, when he was thrust into the family business after the sudden death of his older brother, Alan, in 1973. In the ensuing 30 years, Oke Surfboards has gone full circle: from a business run by three brothers to a large retail and manufacturing operation and back to a small family business. At its peak, Oke employed 13 staff, mostly making boards for other businesses to sell under their own brands.

Family these days consists of Neil and his young adult sons, Daniel and Rory, who honed their board-crafting skills in their mid-teens under their father's watchful eye. Amid the rise of global surf brands and mass-produced boards, Neil is confident that Oke is again doing what it does best – custom-making boards for a small but loyal clientele ranging from talented young surfers to mature longboard riders.

One of Melbourne's last remaining surfboard manufacturers – most have folded or moved to coastal towns – Oke crafts everything from short, high-performance boards to longboards, hybrids and retro designs. Prices start at $550. Working under fluorescent lights in a narrow windowless room, the shaper "reads" the shadows cast on the polyurethane core, carving the required shape and creating a smooth surface. The board is then covered in fibreglass before being resanded, fitted with a removable fin and finally spray-painted by Rory, who designs all of Oke's artwork. Each surfboard takes about eight hours.

With cold beers never far from reach and '70s tracks blaring over the sound of electric sanders, Oke Surfboards' Braeside factory is a hangout for surfers. Some come to catch up with old mates, others simply to watch their board being shaped to their specifications. Neil, who still surfs at weekends, relishes direct contact with his customers. "It is still a thrill for me to see the joy on people's faces when they walk out of here with a new board." *(Oke Surfboards, factory 1, 7 Canterbury Road, Braeside. Full details, page 188.)*

INSPIRATIONS

{ MELBOURNE CRICKET GROUND AND SURROUNDING PARKS }
"It's just an awesome stadium." *(Brunton Avenue, Richmond.)*

{ STATION PIER } "A great place to have fish and chips." *(Port Melbourne.)*

{ BUNNINGS WAREHOUSE, FRANKSTON } "My favourite place for retail therapy." *(Corner McMahon and Gertrude Streets, Frankston, and other locations.)*

OPPOSITE: *Neil Oke's factory has become a hub for surfers.*

JUDY CAMERON

{ TOY MAKER }

In Judy Cameron's bathroom there is a tub piled with bags of toy stuffing, a mountain that almost reaches the ceiling. This, says Judy pointing to the stack, is the best toy stuffing available, giving form to her beautifully made toys – jointed gingham giraffes and teddy bears, classically dressed dolls and colourful spinning mobiles.

It's this finicky attention to unseen details that sets Judy's toys apart. After 20 years in the finance industry, Judy was looking for a career change. It seemed natural to turn her crafting hobby – over the years she had tinkered with everything from smocking and quilting to mosaics – into a full-time job. That was in 1994. Today, her quaintly old-fashioned toys grace the shelves of a select range of children's boutiques and have found their way into countless nurseries.

Her work is evident throughout her home-based studio: old fruit boxes are stacked with fabric in the kitchen, a bookshelf in the sitting room is overrun with more fabric, and the dining area has been given over completely to a work space in which the sewing machine is barely visible among works in progress.

Judy might take up to four hours to complete a doll, including making its costume and stitching in hair. She admits that the activity consumes her – she works through the night, often until four or five in the morning. "I lose myself quite easily in the work. I get such pleasure from seeing something that starts as a flat piece of fabric transformed into a wonderful little character within a couple of hours." *(Stockist details, page 183.)* ✿

INSPIRATIONS

{ MEAT MARKET CRAFT CENTRE } "Great gathering place for craft people with its ongoing exhibitions and workshops." *(42 Courtney Street, North Melbourne.)*

{ MELBOURNE OBSERVATION DECK, RIALTO TOWERS }
"To view Melbourne's ever-changing landscape from the 55th floor."
(525 Collins Street, Melbourne.)

{ HERRING ISLAND ENVIRONMENTAL SCULPTURE PARK } "A wonderful escape in the middle of the Yarra with a gallery, walks and barbecue area." *(Access by punt from Como Landing, Alexander Avenue, South Yarra.)*

OPPOSITE: *Toy maker Judy Cameron loses herself in her work, often stitching until the early hours of the morning.*

LACHLAN FISHER

{ CRICKET BAT MAKER }

Almost 20 years ago, Lachlan Fisher threw in his job as a graphic designer to satisfy a lifelong urge to craft things with his hands. Now one of Australia's best-known cricket bat-makers – or podshavers, as they are known – Lachlan makes about 500 bats a year for clients who range from local amateurs to first-class cricketers. The hours are long and the work is physically demanding, but the former club cricketer and ardent fan of the game still gets a buzz from working the willow.

The craft of podshaving has changed little since the game began. Air-dried English willow – the timber of choice for cricket bats – is selected for the straightness and width of its grain. The wood is pressed to provide a surface capable of withstanding the impact of a hard leather cricket ball, then shaped and balanced until the "pick-up" is right.

Lachlan imports premium English-grown willow to create his bats, but with top-of-the-line Fisher bats now reaching $430, it has become increasingly difficult to compete with cheap Indian-made bats. Fortunately, he has an ace up his sleeve. Recently he began hand-crafting a second range of bats from willow grown in Gippsland, which he fells and dries himself, keeping costs down. The bats, marketed under the Hog Ozblade label but made using the same painstaking methods as his premium product, will be comparable in price to Indian bats.

Lachlan believes his Australian-grown willow could eventually be exported to the lucrative Indian bat-making industry. But this artist-turned-artisan has no plans to stop making bats himself. "It's still the most enjoyable thing I do," he says. "Carving the first bat of the day, I develop sweat, rhythm and perseverance. It's immensely satisfying."
(Fisher Hand-Crafted Cricket Bats, 295a Geelong Road, Kingsville. Full details, page 184.)

INSPIRATIONS

{ NATIONAL GALLERY OF VICTORIA INTERNATIONAL } "Inspiring wood sculpture and landscape painting, in particular, Turner."
(180 St Kilda Road, Melbourne.)

{ STRZELECKI RANGES, GIPPSLAND } "Magnificent country and home to the biggest tree in Australia. A great place to take English visitors."

{ WILLIAMSTOWN } "The whole geography of Williamstown is marvellous. It's a coastal town and you can look across the bay to a city of 3.5 million people. It makes me feel good."

OPPOSITE: *Lachlan Fisher threw in his job as a graphic designer to craft cricket bats.*

Blocks cut 26 Apr 05

ADRIENNE CHISHOLM

{ PUPPET MAKER / DESIGNER }

For as long as she can remember, Adrienne Chisholm has been designing things. Some have been strange – like the three-metre giraffe she crafted as a 10-year-old from milk cartons and papier-mâché, or, more recently, a giant inflatable house, through which synthetic smoke can be pumped, created for the Metropolitan Fire Brigade's community education programs. But these days, the designer and artist spends much of her free time moulding, painting and stitching finger puppets, having been fascinated with puppetry since watching *Sesame Street* as a child.

Adrienne's interest in puppetry developed further when she backpacked through Europe after completing a graphic design degree in 1989. "Puppets are revered and appreciated in countries like Germany, where there is an understanding of the important role they can play in a child's life," she says. It was during a stint as a nanny in London that Adrienne made her first family of puppets, featuring cartoonish hand-moulded clay heads and tiny felt bodies. They were an instant hit with her young charges.

Back home in Australia, Adrienne continued to make puppets to finance her way through a theatre design course at the Victorian College of the Arts. In the ensuing 10 years, her career as a theatre designer, freelance illustrator and theatrical puppet maker has flourished, with high-profile commissions from the Melbourne Theatre Company, the Polyglot Puppet Theatre, and various government organisations.

But her passion for finger puppets remains strong, buoyed by the response she receives from customers young and old. Drawing inspiration from film, children's books and her own design background, her immediately lovable characters include animals, nurses, firefighters and fairytale characters. "You get the most fantastic stories when children put random characters together such as a spaceman and a frog. It really fires their imagination, Adrienne says." *(Contact and stockist details, page 183.)* ❧

INSPIRATIONS

{ THE LITTLE BOOKROOM } "I love going there to look at the books – it's like stepping inside a child's mind." *(771 Nicholson Street, Carlton North.)*

{ CHAPEL STREET BAZAAR } "Great place to fossick around." *(217-223 Chapel Street, Prahran.)*

{ VINTAGE FILMS FROM THE 1930S AND '40S } "For sheer fun and theatricality."

OPPOSITE: *Watching* Sesame Street *as a child stirred Adrienne Chisholm's interest in puppetry.*

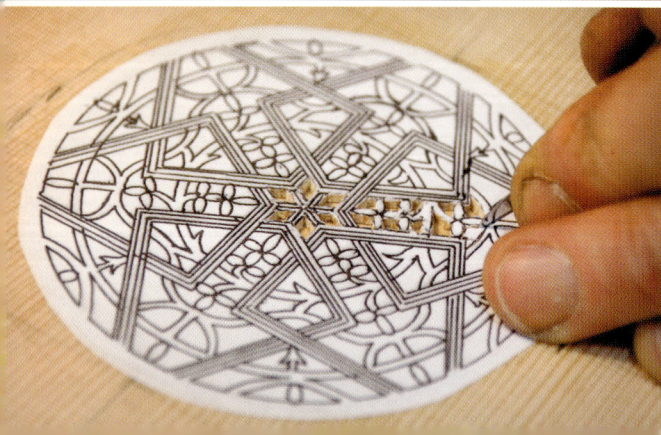

IAN WATCHORN

{ STRINGED INSTRUMENT MAKER }

Ian Watchorn's garden workshop is scattered with a profusion of traditional wood-working tools, pots of varnish, wood shavings and curiously shaped instruments in various stages of completion, including a honey-coloured baroque violin to which Ian is fitting a bridge and tailpiece. It would not be surprising if a musician from the court of Henry VIII entered.

Ian has been making, repairing and conserving historic stringed instruments for the past 30 years. Specialising in instruments and bows from the 16th to the 19th century, he has made lutes, mandolins, guitars, violas da gamba and violins to original designs.

In the 1980s, he studied instrument conservation at the renowned Germanisches Nationalmuseum in Nuremberg, where he became a senior conservator, before returning to Australia to curate the musical instrument collection at Sydney's Powerhouse Museum.

The son of two piano teachers who were also accomplished choirmasters, Ian grew up in Newcastle surrounded by music. Initially he learnt piano, cello and guitar but, in his late teens, he developed an interest in historic instruments. When the local early music group wanted him to become their lute player, Ian could not afford to buy an instrument so instead he built one using a kit. "It was playable but I wasn't happy," he recalls of that first attempt. "I built another one and another one after that ... and I'm still trying to get it right." For historical accuracy, Ian sources most of his wood – maple spruce, fruit woods, cypress – from Europe and mixes his own varnishes using 17th century recipes.

Today, Ian's finely crafted instruments are sought by local and international performers, private collectors and public museums around the world, and his passion for baroque and classical instruments remains undiminished. "There is something quite extraordinary about the creativity of this period. It's a constant source of inspiration." *(Contact details, page 191.)* 🦋

INSPIRATIONS

{ NATIONAL GALLERY OF VICTORIA INTERNATIONAL } "I love going there, among other things, to see a late 18th century portrait of Boccherini playing the cello." *(180 St Kilda Road, Melbourne.)*

{ GRAINGER MUSEUM} "With the right kind of support, it could form the basis of a really good musical instrument collection for Melbourne." *(University of Melbourne, Royal Parade, Parkville.)*

{ALEX W GRANT VIOLINS } "Alex is one of a handful of fine restorers of violins and bows in Melbourne." *(26 Smith Street, Collingwood.)*

OPPOSITE: *Instrument maker Ian Watchorn grew up surrounded by music.*

ALANA WATERSON & SARA DICKINS

{ STATIONERY DESIGNERS }

When Chinese sage Confucius said, "Everything has beauty, but not everyone sees it," he could have been referring to Alana Waterson and Sara Dickins. The duo finds beauty in unexpected places – a leafless branch in winter, a tiny bird in their garden, a bold hydrangea bloom – and translates the images into a charming collection of cards, gift tags and stationery sets.

"Our cards give us the opportunity to express who we are and what we see in a way that celebrates all that is genuine and special about nature," says Alana.

The long-time friends' paths diverged when they left school; Alana studied screen-printing and Sara became a financial controller. Their paths crossed again in 2003, when Alana sought financial advice from her old friend about selling the cards she had produced for an assignment. Eventually, they decided to pair Alana's creative talent with Sara's business acumen to create and market a stationery range under the label Poppies for Grace.

The cards reflect Alana's love of layering. She photographs or paints small images inspired by the natural world, scans them into her computer and manipulates colours and sizes. The printed images are then stitched to heavy cardboard, along with old stamps and colourful paper for extra textural interest. Together, Alana and Sara produce up to 200 items a week, which end up in around 40 stores around the country. Cards range in price from $6.50 to $7.50; boxed cards and tags sell for $24 (set of six) and $33 (12). *(Contact and stockist details, page 191.)* ✿

INSPIRATIONS

{ SPACECRAFT } "We adore and admire their work. The bedding and soft furnishings make us jump up and down – they are truly wonderful." *(Level 1, GPO Melbourne, corner Bourke and Elizabeth Streets, Melbourne; see also page 36.)*

{ RIPE – AUSTRALIAN PRODUCE } "Great homemade food. We go there to dream and plan and go home with full bellies and the confidence to create." *(376 Mount Dandenong Tourist Road, Sassafras.)*

{ LUFT } "Not only is Mark Scholz's store beautiful, but he has nurtured our business – we love him." *(212 St Georges Road, Fitzroy North.)*

OPPOSITE: *Alana Waterson (left) and Sara Dickins have brought together their creative and business talents.*

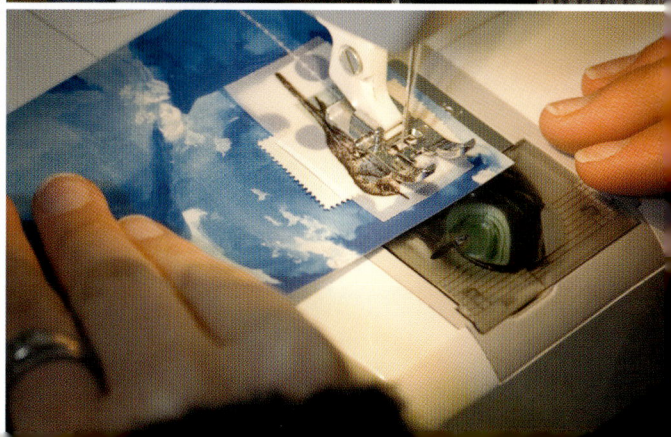

LEON PETROFF

{ VIOLIN MAKER }

Leon Petroff is struggling to explain how the age of a violin can dramatically alter its sound. And so he uses music to illustrate his point, playing Bach's *Violin Concerto in E Major* first on a violin he made in 2003, and then on an instrument made in 1999. The difference is remarkable: the older violin produces a hauntingly warm, mellow tone, compared with the higher pitched resonance of the other.

The master luthier began playing violin as a six-year-old in the western Ukraine city of Lvov, and continued until he graduated from music school at 21. But a fear of performing saw him reject the stage in favour of an apprenticeship with a local violin repairer in 1979. After a violin-maker suggested he try making his own, Leon travelled to Moscow, studying the craft at the Moscow Conservatory of Music for two years. Migrating to Melbourne in 1990, he worked with local luthiers before establishing his own business four years later. In an effort to further refine his skills, Leon spent 1997 studying under Valerio Prilipco in the birthplace of violin-making, Cremona, Italy, and a further few months working with renowned French makers Nicole Dumond and Ghaleb Hassan in Montpellier.

Leon divides his time between repairing and making violins, but thrives on the slow and meticulous process of turning timber into instrument. He begins by selecting the wood (Yugoslavian maple for the back and scroll, Swiss spruce for the top) and ends by applying a 40th coat of varnish. A violin costs $15,500 and may take weeks to complete.

Among his customers are Melbourne Symphony Orchestra associate concertmaster Mark Mogilevski, and internationally renowned violinist and conductor Kek-Tjiang Lim, for whom he repaired a 1715 Domenico Montagnana violin. Leon prides himself on his workmanship and warns customers against asking him to replicate antique instruments: "I don't do copies – I am not Stradivari, I am Petroff." *(Contact details, page 188.)* ✻

INSPIRATIONS

{ JOSEPH EDELMAN, MELBOURNE ARTIST} "I really like his work – he's painted my portrait, and some of his paintings are hung in my shop."

{ LORGEN INTERNATIONAL DELI } "A great place to buy food imported from Russia." *(236 Carlisle Street, Balaclava.)*

{ DAVIS MUSIC CENTRE } "Julie and Lucio (Tony) Ughetti run this wonderful place, which has an extensive range of all sorts of musical instruments." *(27 Byron Street, Footscray.)*

OPPOSITE: *Stage fright turned Leon Petroff from violinist to violin maker.*

DANIEL CHIRICO

{ BAKER }

Intending to study graphic design when he left school, Daniel Chirico instead fell into baking when a baker friend asked him to help out at weekends. While his mates were nightclubbing, this son of a tailor was pursuing the unsociable lifestyle of a baker, mixing dough at some of Melbourne's best-known bakeries. But it was during a working holiday in Europe that Daniel learnt how to make a truly great loaf of bread. After a stint in Italy with a baker of French-style bread, he headed to the historic French town of Montpellier to work under a baker who "revered and respected bread".

Returning to Melbourne in 2001, he opened baker D. Chirico, which these days produces about 5000 loaves a week and supports a staff of 14. The 10 bread varieties, including grainy wholewheat and a dark, cake-like *schwarzbrot*, are all based on Daniel's carefully nurtured apple-based leaven (sourdough starter). Mixed separately, the doughs are allowed to rest for several hours, divided into rounds, rested again, hand-shaped into loaves, rested and allowed to rise again, then baked. The whole process takes about 12 hours, longer in cold weather. "In this bakery, our greatest predator is a draught," says Daniel. Judging the right moment to divide the dough is a key part of the bread-making process. "This is the time that you look at the mixture and reflect as an artisan," he says. Using quality flour is also vital. Daniel sources his from family-run boutique mills in New South Wales and Queensland.

But it is through hand-shaping the bread that Daniel feels most connected to his product – a connectedness he hopes to pass on to his customers. "Of all food, bread is the thing that really connects people to the land. People who are drawn to this bakery come here not only for the bread, but to see and smell how something is produced." *(baker D. Chirico, 149 Fitzroy Street, St Kilda. Full details page 183.)* ❧

INSPIRATIONS

{ SOMEDAY GALLERY} "I absolutely relate to the aesthetic of this gallery and retail space, which supports up-and-coming artisans." *(Level 3b, Curtin House, 252 Swanston Street, Melbourne.)*

{ AUSTRALIAN CENTRE FOR CONTEMPORARY ART } "Beautiful works, beautiful space." *(111 Sturt Street, Southbank.)*

{ INDUSTRIA } "The owners are passionate about what they do and have some great stuff." *(202 Gertrude Street, Fitzroy.)*

OPPOSITE: *It is through hand-shaping his bread that Daniel Chirico feels most connected to his product.*

GRACIA HABY
& LOUISE JENNISON

{ JOURNAL MAKERS / ARTISTS }

As two of the Melbourne art scene's emerging talents, Gracia Haby and Louise Jennison have filled hundreds of sketchbooks with their drawings and notes. Known for both individual and collaborative works on paper – mainly drawings and collages featuring subjects as diverse as extinct animals and everyday garden scenes – each has had work exhibited in galleries around Australia and overseas.

But it was the pair's search for the perfect journal – one that would lie flat, enabling sketching right into the spine – that led to the creation of hammer & daisy. Using skills they learnt during a month-long scholarship at the specialist bookbinding school Centro del bel Libro in Ascona, Switzerland, Gracia and Louise started their journal-making business in 2003.

Today, they create not only journals but complementary accessories such as journal pouches and pencil cases. Prices range from about $5.50 for a fabric-covered notebook, to around $180 for a limited-edition display album. Louise and Gracia make the journals in three sizes, each with 25 sheets of archival-quality paper that are bound using a painstakingly slow, traditional method of tying small square knots – 164 knots for an A4 journal – over and through brass wire and rods to form a flexible spine. They go to great lengths to source unusual fabrics to cover the journals, ranging from a 1950s' Hungarian tea towel discovered in a secondhand shop to a vintage skirt unearthed at a local market. Each journal takes about three weeks to complete. But in sharing the workload, the pair might have up to 40 journals under way at a time in their inner-city studio. Devotees of the journals include fellow artists, who use them as sketchbooks, and new mothers, who record special memories from their children's early years in the carefully bound pages. *(Contact details, page 185.)* ❀

INSPIRATIONS

{ HOUND DOG'S BOP SHOP } Original and reissued recordings of rock 'n' roll, rockabilly, country, blues, soul, jive and boogie.
(313 Victoria Street, West Melbourne.)

{ THE GREVILLE STREET BOOKSTORE } A huge selection of design books, international magazine titles and hard-to-find fanzines.
(145 Greville Street, Prahran.)

{ STICKY } This subterranean arcade is an appropriate place to find a store devoted to zines (experimental self-published magazines) and artist books.
(Shop 10, Campbell Arcade, Melbourne.)

OPPOSITE: *Gracia Haby (left) and Louise Jennison's journals can each take up to three weeks to complete.*

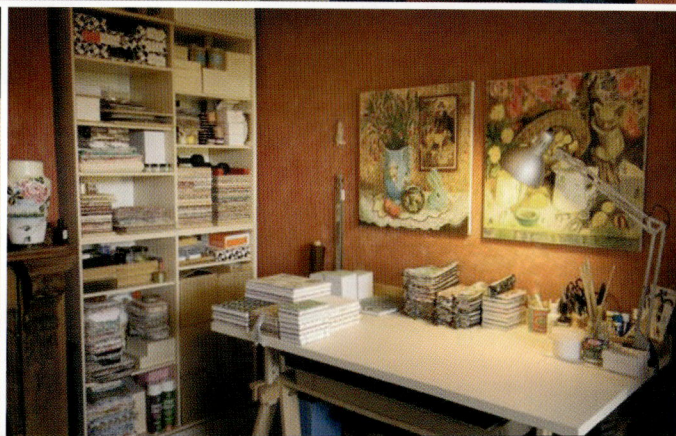

CAROLYN IMLACH

{ SOAP MAKER }

Walking into Est is like falling head-first into a giant perfume bottle. Even before you reach the shop door, the aroma of essential oils pervades the air. Once inside, apron-clad Carolyn Imlach is just visible in the tiny workroom at the rear of the store. It is day six in the soap-making process and Carolyn is blending geranium, lavender and lemon oils into a thick olive oil mixture, which is just beginning to cure. It is a critical stage in the production process and one that Carolyn rarely entrusts to anyone else. "I can tell immediately if something needs a little bit more lavender or a little less geranium," she says.

When the soap has fully cured (a process that can take up to 10 days, depending on the weather), it is rolled into balls, each bearing the fingerprints of its maker. It is physically demanding work but Carolyn finds the process meditative.

The former textile product manager turned to soap-making when she was made redundant several years ago. Having spent hours in the State Library researching traditional soap-making methods, Carolyn combined her love of cooking and an interest in olive oil to develop a range of soaps, lip balms, salves and bath oils, which she initially sold at weekend markets. Now, Est Australia products are sold at more than 100 Australian retail outles as well as in the United Kingdom, Singapore and Hong Kong. All are handmade using Australian extra virgin olive oil and, where possible, unrefined natural and organic ingredients.

When not making soap, Carolyn is kept busy visiting the many artisans who supply her shop with a beguiling mix of handmade products, many made to her specifications.
The products include finger-knitted sisal bags from Tasmania, nail brushes made from plant fibre, and delicious caramels sourced from a tiny village in rural France.
(Est Australia, 134 Auburn Road, Hawthorn East. Full details, page 186.) ✻

INSPIRATIONS

Mixing, stirring, rolling, sealing

{ MELBOURNE'S YARRA RIVER } "Running the bush tracks along the Boulevard removes me from the noise and chaos and gives me time to reflect. When you are in a still place it allows ideas to flow."

{ STEP BACK ANTIQUES } "I go there for props for the shop. Jane and Deborah are passionate about what they do and find the most amazing stuff."
(103 Burwood Road, Hawthorn.)

{ H LEFFLER & SON LEATHER MERCHANTS} "It makes you feel like you want to create something when you walk in here. Lots of interesting leather, buckles and cowhides." *(50-66 York Street, South Melbourne.)*

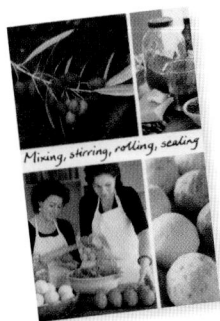

OPPOSITE: *Carolyn Imlach finds the process of rolling soap balls meditative.*

Est
A more soulful life

change all things you
fashion with a breath
of your own spirit

Est
OLIVE OIL SOAP
EST AUSTRALIA PTY LTD

ARNO BACKES

{ CHOCOLATIER }

Several chocolate lovers have their noses pressed to Koko Black's shop window, watching Arno Backes at work. Looking every bit the master chocolatier in his tall, pleated chef's hat, German-born Arno is mid-way through tempering a batch of Callebaut couverture, gently stirring the mixture over a bain-marie to stabilise the cocoa butter crystals. It's a tricky process. A tiny temperature variation at this stage would spoil the chocolate, making it less shiny and far too malleable. But Arno can tell at a glance when it is ready to be sculpted or poured into moulds.

Arno knew he wanted to work with chocolate at 15, when he was apprenticed to a pastry chef in St Wendel, a small town in southwestern Germany. "The Germans take chocolate very seriously," he says. "It's just such a beautiful subject to work with." Completing a masters degree as a pastry chef/chocolatier in 1996, he honed his skills with some of Europe's top chocolatiers and sugar artists. A highlight was receiving a thank-you note from Queen Elizabeth II, for whom he made chocolates while working for Marasu's Petits Fours in London. In 2004, Arno moved to Australia, working as a sugar artist for Koko Black's sister company, Suga, before taking up his current role as head chocolatier.

More rational scientist than whimsical Willy Wonka, Arno says it can take up to six months to develop a single product, such as an orange and Cointreau truffle. New products are tested for texture, shine and snap before customers and staff are invited to provide feedback.

Many would view his as the dream job but the question has to be asked: does he ever tire of chocolate? "Not if it is made by a craftsman," he insists. "I get nervous if I don't have any." *(Koko Black, shop 4, Royal Arcade, 335 Bourke Street, Melbourne, and other locations. Full details, page 182.)* 🍫

INSPIRATIONS

{ QUEEN VICTORIA MARKET } "The choice and quality of the nuts and fruits is amazing and the atmosphere is buzzing." *(Corner Elizabeth and Victoria Streets, Melbourne.)*

{ SUGA } "Being a former sugar artist myself, I admire the work and craft of the product." *(Shop 20, Royal Arcade, 335 Bourke Street, Melbourne, and other locations.)*

{ RIDING MY MOTORCYCLE IN THE HILLS OF VICTORIA } "For the fresh air and the scenery."

OPPOSITE: *Arno Backes knew he wanted to work with chocolate when he was 15.*

JACK SPIRA

{ GUITAR MAKER }

Jack Spira's cramped and rustic workspace, overlooking paddocks of grazing cows and recently ploughed fields, is strewn with instruments in various stages of completion. Looking around, it's hard to believe that some of these creations might make their way into the hands of some of the world's best-known musicians. Sting owns four Spira guitars (the former Police frontman asked him to reproduce a favourite early 1900s Martin guitar), and Australian music duo Deborah Conway and Willy Zygier swear by his work.

Jack began making banjos and guitars while studying sculpture at university. He left Australia in the late 1980s to learn musical instrument technology at the London College of Furniture, returning in 1991 to set up a small guitar-making business. He began by selling his instruments at folk festivals, gaining commissions from those who saw and loved his work. "I could build guitars of a professional standard, but really needed to take my work to the next stage," he recalls. It was customers who helped refine his skills – their pedantic requests proved valuable learning tools.

Jack builds up to 20 guitars, bouzoukis and mandolins a year, half of which are sold to customers in America, Singapore and Japan. "I am very fussy with timbers – they can not have any flaws or faults," he says, adding that he prefers to use sustainable timbers, which he dries and ages himself. As all instruments are made to order, no two are alike. Each takes up to eight weeks to complete and sells for around $3000. "I never chose to be an instrument maker. It chose me. It took about 10 years before I finally realised this was what I was born to do." *(Contact details, page 190.)* ⚒

INSPIRATIONS

{ TOTALLY GOURDGEOUS } "This is a really cool band that plays instruments made from gourds crafted by Penelope Swales." *(Contact details, page 190.)*

{ CHRIS WYNNE, GUITAR MAKER } "Chris offers great guitar-making tuition through Thomas Lloyd Guitars, based at Montsalvat in Eltham." *(Contact details, page 191.)*

{ NATIVE AUSTRALIAN TIMBER ART } "It's the only venue in central Melbourne that I'm aware of where an artisan like me can exhibit work." *(Shop 5, 1 Exhibition Street, Melbourne.)*

OPPOSITE: *Jack Spira started out selling his guitars at folk festivals; now musicians such as Sting seek out his work.*

JANE WIFFEN

{ CUPCAKE MAKER }

To perfect her tiny cupcakes, Jane Wiffen spent three months in 2005 holed up in her kitchen, tweaking old recipes and blending icing using colour-mixing advice she had sought from artists, until finally she was satisfied that she had created the definitive bite-sized morsel. Jane, whose background was in fashion retail, had spent years dreaming of making cupcakes that would be to baking what Chanel was to fashion. They had to be feminine and alluring, she decided; a mouthful of pure chic.

Today, Jane's Addiction Cakes can be found nestled in race-goers' hampers, as *bonbonnière* gifts at weddings, and gracing the birthday tables of pint-sized suburban princesses. Jane finds inspiration for her decorations in everything from the pastel hues of a lingerie set to the embroidered flower on a handbag or a boldly coloured vase. Butter-cream icing, hand-tinted to order, provides the foundation on which Jane positions flowers fashioned from royal icing and dipped in edible glitter, tiny piped beads or silver cachous.

Jane's production process is like a time-and-motion study. Each tiny creation takes about seven minutes to decorate, excluding the time spent crafting the adornments and baking the cakes. There can be a downside to Jane's pursuit of perfection. Weeks went by as she trialled cupcakes with chocolate truffle centres. "I had to keep taste-testing them to make sure I got them right," she says. "I gained almost 10 kilos." *(Contact and stockist details, page 191.)* ✿

INSPIRATIONS

{ CHRISTINE } This basement store is like Aladdin's cave, stuffed with fabulous jewellery, bags, and accessories. *(181 Flinders Lane, Melbourne.)*

{ EXHIBIT INTERIORS } Interesting Australian-designed furniture, glassware and ceramics, plus unusual Italian lighting. *(Shop 67-69 Collins Place, Exhibition Street, Melbourne.)*

{ CENTRAL STATION RECORDS } A huge range of imported and home-grown hip-hop, R&B and dance music. *(2 Somerset Place, Melbourne.)*

OPPOSITE: *Jane Wiffen spent three months holed up in her kitchen to perfect her cupcake recipe.*

ANITA MIKEDIS

{ BOTANICAL HOMEWARES DESIGNER }

Who would have thought that a few eucalypt leaves, a handful of cardamom pods and a bunch of cinnamon sticks could deliver a sensory pleasure greater than the sum of its parts? But by tucking the leaves and aromatic spices into separate hand-sewn pockets of creamy organza, Anita Mikedis's Evexia botanical sachets become exquisite tokens too beautiful and fragrant to tuck away in a drawer. Unlike potpourri, which combines dried leaves and flowers to create a scented mixture, Anita prefers to keep her scents separate. One sheer pocket might contain a single slice of dried orange and another dried bay leaves, while a spice sachet will match individual pockets of cinnamon with others of star anise and cardamom.

Tired of the "figures and number crunching" involved in fashion, and with an awakening interest in aromatherapy, the former clothing designer established Evexia in 2000. Today, her small home-based workroom abounds with sacks of organic wheat, used to fill wheat pillows, and bags of air-dried leaves and petals. Anita gathers her ingredients from a range of sources, including a verbena plant farm in central Victoria, gum trees in a friend's backyard and oriental spice stores. Many she dries herself.

Evexia botanical sachets range in price from $16 to $26, hand-poured soy wax candles sell for around $36, wheat pillows made from vintage fabrics for $34 and soaps wrapped in Japanese paper start at $7.50. Sitting in her workroom, delicately scented with spice and eucalyptus from one of her candles, Anita says that what she loves best about her work now is the sensory aspect. "Something made by hand and with heart touches the soul. It has integrity."
(Contact and stockist details, page 188.) 🌿

INSPIRATIONS

{ CERES COMMUNITY ENVIRONMENT PARK } "Their work with sustainability and fair trade inspires me to be more earth-conscious about the products I create, hence my use of recycled fabrics, natural botanicals and minimal packaging." *(8 Lee Street, Brunswick East.)*

{ INDUSTRIA } "This unusual business's obscure collectibles might include old signs, lab equipment and vintage school geography maps." *(202 Gertrude Street, Fitzroy.)*

{ EMPIRE VINTAGE } "I love the way this delightfully eccentric shop, which sells everything from lingerie to homewares, gives new life to objects from the past." *(63 Cardigan Place, Albert Park.)*

OPPOSITE: *Anita Mikedis gathers her ingredients from sources such as friends' backyards and oriental spice stores.*

JOANNE SCHOOF

{ CANDLE MAKER }

Midway through a bus trip around rural Spain in the late 1990s, Joanne Schoof had an epiphany. Intrigued by the work of Spanish chandlers and inspired by the people, places and lifestyles she had encountered while backpacking, she realised then and there that craft, and candle-making specifically, was her calling.

Intending to become a graphic designer, Joanne trained in art and design after leaving school in 1997. But craft was in her blood. Her grandmother wove carpets and rugs on a loom that filled a bedroom, while her mother had always been able to knit or sew "just about anything". Joanne returned to Melbourne to research candle-making, pouring her first candles at her parents' kitchen stove. She has since moved to a makeshift workshop – previously the garden shed – in her family's outer-suburban backyard. The workshop, dwarfed by gum trees, is strewn with colourful stalagmites of dribbled wax, a study in organised chaos. "I can always find what I want even if no one else can," says Joanne, who increasingly has to call on friends for help to meet the demand for her products.

Rather than emulate the techniques of master chandlers, who aspire to produce flawless candles, Joanne embraces textural imperfection. She developed a cold-pour technique designed to trap air bubbles in the wax, so producing a wonderfully craggy surface that begs to be touched. Joanne makes her own latex moulds cast from natural objects such as pumpkins and river stones or designs her own. She favours simple shapes, which, grouped together, take on a new significance and strength. *(Contact and stockist details, page 190.)* ✿

INSPIRATIONS

a little light

{ HERMON & HERMON } "I think Barbara Hermon must be my fairy godmother. She saw the potential in what I do and had the vision to present it to her customers." *(556 Swan Street, Richmond.)*

{ ST ANDREWS MARKET } "The ultimate way to spend a Saturday morning – surrounded by gum trees, drumbeats, dancing and delicious food." *(Saturdays, corner Kangaroo Ground and St Andrews Roads, St Andrews.)*

{ NATIONAL GALLERY OF VICTORIA AUSTRALIA } "I love the Australian collection, particularly works by the Heidelberg School. They did a lot of their paintings around the area where I grew up, and I just feel such a connection to the bush as they capture it. If I ever have a spare hour, I can't help but to pop in." *(Corner Russell and Flinders Streets, Melbourne.)*

OPPOSITE: *Natural shapes such as pumpkins or river stones inspire Joanne Schoof's candles.*

PETER LANCASTER

{ LITHOGRAPHER }

Peter Lancaster admits it took a leap of faith to set up his lithography studio in 1990. After all, who in their right mind would establish a business whose survival depended on the patronage of cash-strapped artists? But Peter's passion for stone lithography was such that he felt he had no choice. Introduced to the craft while studying a fine arts degree, he was hooked "from the moment I put crayon to stone". After completing a master printer traineeship at New Mexico's internationally renowned centre for fine art lithography, the Tamarind Institute, Peter returned to Australia and established Lancaster Press, now based in an airy studio behind his home.

Stone lithography was developed as a commercial printing process in Germany in the 18th century. Artists gradually came to realise that the process was an effective way to create multiple images and, for the past 150 years, lithography has been used to create fine art prints, which are considered original works of art. Lithographic printing relies on the principle that oil and water do not mix. At the outset, an artist draws on a smooth, porous surface (traditionally Bavarian limestone) with oily crayons. The image is fixed with gum arabic and nitric acid and the stone rinsed clean. Greasy ink sticks to the crayoned areas and runs off the wet stone. When paper is placed on the stone and run through a press, the inked image is transferred to paper.

Peter has collaborated with prominent and emerging artists, among them John Coburn, Mirka Mora and Jon Cattapan. He relishes discovering how their work will translate into print and they enjoy having to think about their art in a differet way. Lithography results in striking textures and effects. Highly illustrative or graphic work tends to respond best but even then, there is a risk that images will drop out or lose subtleties. "It's almost as though there is a litho-god," says Peter. "There is such mystery to it. Sometimes things work, other times they don't. It's forever challenging." (*Contact details, page 187.*) ✳

INSPIRATIONS

{ RUBBLE AND RICHES MARKET } New and second-hand goods "with a crazy mix of people". (*8 Leakes Road, Laverton.*)

{ ST KILDA BOWLING CLUB } "Like an old smoky lounge room – something that hasn't changed in an area where everything has changed."
(*66 Fitzroy Street, St Kilda.*)

{ SURFING AT PHILLIP ISLAND } "I enjoy the solitude of surfing here and separating myself from my work."

OPPOSITE: *Peter Lancaster in his lithography studio; the Bavarian limestone slabs (bottom left) upon which artists draw to start the process.*

DAVID COLES

{ PAINT MAKER }

David Coles has messed about with paint since he was a child. He recalls being fascinated by the tiny jars of pure pigment ("little jewels of colour") that his mother brought home from the family-run art supplies shop. Today, this fine arts graduate remains captivated by the stuff. "I'm just seduced by the richness and textures of all the materials I work with," enthuses this modern-day colourman, who paints in his spare time.

Visiting Australia in 1994 while on a break from his job as a paint specialist with a British art supplies firm, David realised there was a gap in the local market for premium art materials. Moving to Melbourne within months of that visit, he set up Langridge Artist Colours to make materials for artists and artisans, including instrument-makers, gilders and decorators. Working from a factory in the city's inner west, David and three staff use top-grade materials to mix paints, varnishes, waxes and resins by hand. The pure pigments, some dating back to ancient times, are sourced from all over the world. David cautiously removes the lid from a tin marked "Prussian blue" – one of the first "modern" colours, created in 1704. Inside is a shimmering powder that appears almost to float.

Turning pigment into paint is a labour-intensive process requiring concentration and diligence. David mixes the pigment with oil to form a paste, and then runs it through a mill, adjusting it manually to ensure that every particle of pigment is evenly coated with oil. Making 10 litres of paint can take up to eight hours. But for David, it is time well spent. He derives great satisfaction from seeing his paints in use. "But in the end, the materials are only tools. It is the artist that actually takes those tools and creates a work of art with them." *(Contact details, page 183.)* ✿

INSPIRATIONS

{ NIAGARA GALLERIES } "Look no further than here for quality contemporary art with lots of paint!" *(245 Punt Road, Richmond.)*

{ AUSTRALIAN PRINT WORKSHOP } "Art print editions with a great collection of affordable prints, all done on-site in the rear workshop. Courses available as well." *(210 Gertrude Street, Fitzroy.)*

{ THE OLD VILLAGE LOLLIE SHOP } "Old-school sweet shop. Many British traditional chocolates and lollies. Perfect!" *(51 Anderson Street, Yarraville.)*

OPPOSITE: *David Coles sources his pure pigments from all over the world.*

EMMA COWAN

{ CARD DESIGNER / ARTIST }

Sitting in her small studio, sun streaming through the window, Emma Cowan is explaining what sets her cards apart from the thousands on sale in supermarkets, service stations and milk bars. Hers have an elegance and intelligence about them, she says. Small wonder. Emma majored in painting at Auckland University's Elam School of Fine Arts and her artistic training is evident in the clever use of colour, delicate artwork and textural finishes that she brings to her small, one-of-a-kind collages.

Moving from New Zealand to Australia in 2000, Emma looked for a small business that would generate enough income to support her work as an artist. She had dabbled in card-making in New Zealand and decided to deploy the box of beautiful papers and sewing machine that had accompanied her across the Tasman.

She begins each batch of cards by sifting through her stockpile of cardboard, colourful paper and printed ephemera – old French posters, German *Vogue* magazines from the 1960s and Eastern European stamps. Sometimes she dips into her collection of drawings, fabric and the handwritten journals she finds in second-hand shops. Once she has gathered the various elements, Emma composes her designs – an old newspaper article overlaid with a piece of sheer organza on one; a series of mismatched fabrics on another – then stitches them on to heavyweight card. She makes envelopes by folding then sewing paper.

It's the use of recycled material that most inspires Emma: "The history and personality from the past on each of these cards gives them a special appeal." *(Contact and stockist details, page 183.)* ❧

INSPIRATIONS

{ SYBER'S BOOKS } "A great second-hand bookstore that has a constantly evolving collection. I love browsing through its collection of literature, natural history and old and rare books." *(668 Glenhuntly Road, Caulfield South, and 38 Chapel Street, Windsor.)*

{ STICKY } "This tiny store stocks hundreds of handmade and limited-edition poetry and art books, postcards and handmade zines (self-published newsletters)." *(Shop 10, Campbell Arcade, Melbourne.)*

{ KAZARI WAREHOUSE } "I love hunting through this place, which ships in second-hand treasures from Japan, including beautiful old fabrics and kimonos that have been hand-mended, and beautiful antique furniture." *(7-11 Hill Street, Richmond.)*

OPPOSITE: *Emma Cowan starts the card-making process by sifting through her stockpile of printed ephemera, including old Vogue magazines.*

IRWIN AND McLAREN BOOKBINDERS

{ BOOKBINDERS }

Dusty, inky and cluttered, the Irwin and McLaren studio exudes history. Antique hand tools, passed down through several generations, are still used in bookbinding techniques that have not changed since the family firm was founded more than a century ago. Flour paste is mixed in-house, just as it always has been, and used to glue fine leather to book covers. Other books are covered in buckram (stiff woven linen), their spines stitched or held together with ribbon or screws before being finished with decorative extras such as gold foil debossing, in which type is pressed into the cover and filled with gold foil.

The McLarens have been involved with printing and graphic art since 1871, opening their own manufacturing stationery business in Melbourne's CBD in 1903. Fellow stationer Gordon Irwin became a partner in 1938 but sold out six weeks later. Today, Robert McLaren, great-great grandson of founder James, is the last McLaren still practising the family trade in the inner-city premises that have been the company's home since 1961. He works with a small team of artisans to meet a wide range of client requests, including restoring rare books (such as two valuable 120-year-old volumes on Victorian Aborigines), binding corporate tender documents, crafting leather-bound wedding albums, and making menu covers. Some people have been clients of the firm for more than two generations.

Robert specialises in the 2000-year-old art of marbling, floating pigments on liquid and manipulating the pigments into swirling patterns, which are transferred to paper. The marbled pages are traditionally used as end papers, joining the book block to the front and back cover. Creating books using such time-honoured – and time-consuming – methods is a cumulative process, but to Robert, the work is vital for historical and aesthetic reasons. "Skills such as bookbinding must be maintained if we are to have authentic art available for future generations to see." *(Irwin and McLaren Bookbinders, 64 Cubitt Street, Richmond. Full details, page 186.)* ✳

INSPIRATIONS

{ RENAISSANCE BOOKBINDING } "Proprietor Nick Doslov is an expert in traditional and modern bookbinding. He's a superb craftsman." *(493 Brunswick Street, Fitzroy North.)*

{ TIFFANY POLLARD, JEWELLER } "Tiffany uses traditional goldsmithing methods to create products of amazing quality." *(Contact details, page 189.)*

{ EAST AND WEST ART GALLERY } "This studio/gallery is a great place to find Japanese woodblock prints and Chinese ceramics." *(665 High Street, Kew East.)*

OPPOSITE: *Irwin and McLaren staff members (from left) Phil Ridgway, Andrew Nunns (obscured), Abby Seymour and Storm Pedersen at work.*

JOANNE SAUNDERS

{ RECORDER MAKER }

The mellow sound of a baroque recorder wafts through the draughty corridors of Abbotsford Convent. Ensconced in a small workshop in the gothic-style main building, Joanne Saunders is testing her latest creation by playing one of Bach's *Brandenburg Concertos*. While pleased with the way the instrument is sounding, it will take many hours of "playing in" before the recorder is ready for its new owner, acclaimed French player Hugo Reyne.

Joanne crafts each recorder to an accuracy of up to one 20th of a millimetre using specially designed hand tools, many of which she makes herself. Working on several instruments at a time, each takes up to six weeks to complete, beginning as a block of hardwood that is turned, bored and reamed. Many hours are then spent hand-carving and "voicing" the instrument until Joanne is satisfied with the result.

From an early age, Joanne tinkered in the family workshop, learning woodworking skills from her father, who restored antiques at weekends. Attending Preshil, an alternative school, she learned woodturning, and studied the recorder and oboe. By 15, she knew that she wanted to make recorders for a living and, after studying oboe at the Victorian College of the Arts, Joanne persuaded world-renowned Melbourne recorder-maker Fred Morgan to train her. Later, she set up her own workshop, initially in Daylesford, and then in Melbourne after working as a recorder-maker in Europe for three years. In 2005 she moved to Abbotsford Convent.

Her renaissance and baroque recorders, based on 15th and 16th century instruments housed in European museums and made from Honduras rosewood, European boxwood and the Australian hardwood mulga, are sought by professional musicians around the world, including Australian virtuoso Genevieve Lacey. A part-time oboe and recorder teacher, Joanne describes hearing her instruments played by top performers as the "ultimate experience – a sublime gift to the auditory senses". *(Contact details, page 189.)* ❧

INSPIRATIONS

{ NATIONAL GALLERY OF VICTORIA INTERNATIONAL } "Walking through the NGV, I feel inspired by the design of the refurbished building and the beautiful objects within." *(180 St Kilda Road, Melbourne.)*

{ ABBOTSFORD CONVENT } "A beautiful environment that is perfect for a fusion of creative minds." *(1 St Heliers Street, Abbotsford.)*

{ JUST TOOLS } "Good helpful advice and beautifully designed precision tools." *(180 Clarendon Street, South Melbourne.)*

OPPOSITE: *Joanne Saunders in her Abbotsford Convent studio.*

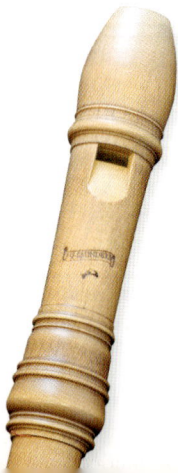

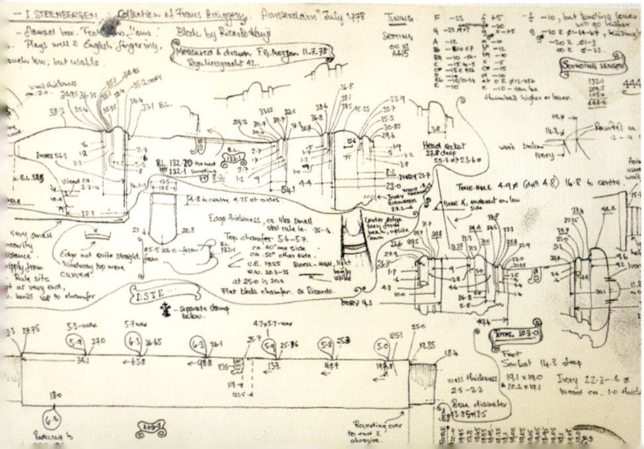
I. STEENBERGEN. Collection of Frans Brüggen. Amsterdam July 1978
Measured & drawn F.G. Morgan 11.7.78
Regulierssgracht 42.
Plays well & English fingering.
TUNING
SETTING
SOUNDING LENGTH
Head socket
thumbhole higher or lower

HANDMADE DIRECTORY

ABBOTSFORD CONVENT,
1 St Heliers Street, Abbotsford T *03 9417 3363*

**ABBOTSFORD SALVATION ARMY
FAMILY STORE,**
81 Victoria Crescent, Abbotsford T *03 9419 7410*

ALICE EUPHEMIA,
*shop 6, Cathedral Arcade, 37 Swanston Street,
Melbourne* W *www.aliceeuphemia.com*

ANTHONY, PAUL – FASHION DESIGNER
Paul Anthony Designs, 81a Chapel Street, Windsor
T *03 9521 4005* W *www.paulanthonydesigns.com*

APRILMAY,
107 Scotchmer Street, Fitzroy North T *03 9489 3004*
W *www.aprilmay.com.au*

ARTISAN BOOKS,
159 Gertrude Street, Fitzroy T *03 9416 4805*
W *www.artisan.com.au*

ART STRETCHERS,
76 Victoria Street, Carlton T *03 9663 8624*
W *www.artspectrum.com.au*

ASSIN,
Basement 138 Little Collins Street, Melbourne
T *03 9654 0158*

ATELIER PUGLISI
see **PUGLISI, BENEDICT G**

**AUSTRALIAN CENTRE FOR
CONTEMPORARY ART,**
111 Sturt Street, Southbank T *03 9697 9999*
W *www.accaonline.org.au*

AUSTRALIAN PRINT WORKSHOP,
210 Gertrude Street, Fitzroy T *03 9419 5466*
W *www.australianprintworkshop.com*

BACKES, ARNO – CHOCOLATIER
*Koko Black, shop 4, Royal Arcade, 335 Bourke Street,
Melbourne* T *03 9639 8911; 167 Lygon Street, Carlton*
T *03 9349 2775; and shop B 118, Chadstone Shopping
Centre, 1341 Dandenong Road, Chadstone*
T *03 9530 9060* W *www.kokoblack.com*

THE BEAD COMPANY OF VICTORIA,
336 Smith Street, Collingwood T *03 9419 0636*
E *beadcovic@bigpond.com.au*

BEAUFORT'S BIG GARAGE SALE,
31 Neill Street, Beaufort (near Ballarat)
T *03 5349 2771 Open daily*

**BEGG, NATALIE –
LINGERIE/FASHION DESIGNER**
Natalie Begg Australia T *03 9388 0455*
E *sales@nataliebegg.com* W *www.nataliebegg.com
Stockists include Smitten Kitten (see listing);
Loving Promises, shop 1, 18 Qantas Domestic
Terminal, Tullamarine Airport* T *03 9310 4461; and
O'Donnells, 437 Chapel Street, South Yarra*
T *03 9827 4700*

BENNETTS LANE JAZZ CLUB,
25 Bennetts Lane, Melbourne T *03 9663 2856*

BISTRIN'S EMPORIUM,
201 Gertrude Street, Fitzroy T *03 9416 0095*

BOULTON, KATE – BUTTON MAKER
*Buttonmania, level 2, Nicholas Building,
37 Swanston Street, Melbourne* T *03 9650 3627*

BOWERBIRD SAVED TIMBERS,
*Old Millgrove Sawmill, 3045 Warburton Highway,
Millgrove, Upper Yarra Valley* T *03 5966 5966*
E *info@bowerbirdtimber.com*
W *www.bowerbirdtimber.com*

BOY & GIRL TOY SHOP,
495 High Street, Prahran T *03 9525 0300*

BUNNINGS WAREHOUSE,
*corner McMahon and Gertrude Streets, Frankston;
3 Nepean Highway, Mentone; and other locations*
W *www.bunnings.com.au*

**BURKIN, GWENDOLYNNE –
FASHION DESIGNER**
*Gwendolynne, 71 Kerr Street, Fitzroy (by
appointment or open Saturday 11.30am – 4.30pm)*
T *03 9415 7687* E *gwendolynneburkin@yahoo.com*

BUTTONMANIA,
see **BOULTON, KATE**

THE BUTTON SHOP,
181 Glenferrie Road, Malvern T *03 9509 7077*

CAINES, JULIE – TASSEL MAKER
Ornamenta Designs T *03 9495 6359*
E *ornamentadesigns@ozemail.com.au Stockist
information Goatham and Associates, 456 High Street,
Prahran East* T *03 9521 3044*

CAMBERWELL SUNDAY MARKET,
Station Street, Camberwell T *1300 367 712*
W *www.sundaymarket.com.au*

CAMERON, JUDY – TOY MAKER
Stockists include Heather Brown, 115 Maling Road, Canterbury T *03 9830 4573; Miko Beautiful Child, 980a Main Road, Eltham* T *03 9439 4888; and Twiggywinkle, 15 Morey Street, Armadale* T *03 9500 0098*

CATTELL, JAMES – TOY MAKER/SCULPTOR
Honeyweather & Speight, 113 Barkly Street, St Kilda T *03 9534 3380* W *www.honeyweatherandspeight.com.au Stockists include Makers Mark Melbourne, 464 Collins Street, Melbourne* T *03 9621 2488 and 88 Collins Street, Melbourne* T *03 9650 3444 Also by commission*

CENTRAL STATION RECORDS,
2 Somerset Place, Melbourne T *03 9642 5744* W *www.centralstationrec.com*

CERES COMMUNITY ENVIRONMENT PARK,
8 Lee Street, Brunswick East T *03 9387 2609* W *www.ceres.org.au*

CHAPEL STREET BAZAAR,
217-223 Chapel Street, Prahran T *03 9529 1727*

CHAPMAN, GEORGIA – FASHION DESIGNER
Vixen, T *03 9417 6322* E *info@vixenaustralia.com* W *www.vixenaustralia.com. Stockists include Andrea Gold, 104 Bridge Road, Richmond* T *03 9428 1226; Blondies (Camberwell, Clifton Hill, Port Melbourne); and Husk (see listing)*

CHARLESWORTH, ANNA – METAL ARTIST
59 Albemarle Street, Williamstown T *03 9397 4222*

CHIRICO, DANIEL – BAKER
baker D. Chirico, 149 Fitzroy Street, St Kilda T *03 9534 3777 Stockists include Passionfoods, 219 Ferrars Street, South Melbourne* T *03 9690 9339; Ripe Organics, shop 7, Prahran Market, Prahran* T *03 9804 8606; and Organica, shop 3, rear 546 Malvern Road, Prahran* T *03 9510 6787*

CHISHOLM, ADRIENNE – PUPPET MAKER/DESIGNER
M *0402 837 839 Stockists Boy & Girl Toy Shop, 495 High Street, Prahran* T *03 9525 0300 and Seagulls Bookshop, 141 Nelson Place, Williamstown* T *03 9397 1728*

CHRISTINE,
181 Flinders Lane, Melbourne T *03 9654 2011*

CITY LIBRARY,
253 Flinders Lane, Melbourne T *03 9664 0800* W *www.citylibrary.org.au*

CITY OF PORT PHILLIP LIBRARIES
corner Montague Street and Dundas Place, Albert Park, and other locations W *www.portphillip.vic.gov.au/about_libraries.html*

COAD, KRIS – CERAMICIST
T *03 9690 6510* M *0403 918719* E *kriscoad@netspace.net.au* W *www.kriscoad.com Stockists include Craft Victoria (see listing) and TarraWarra Museum of Art, 311 Healesville-Yarra Glen Road, Healesville* T *03 5957 3100* W *www.twma.com.au Also by commission*

COLES, DAVID – PAINT MAKER
Langridge Artist Colours T *03 9689 0577* E *info@langridgecolours.com* W *www.langridgecolours.com*

COLLECTED WORKS BOOKSHOP,
level 1, Nicholas Building, 37 Swanston Street, Melbourne T *03 9654 8873* W *www.collectedworks.com.au*

COLLINGWOOD CHILDREN'S FARM,
St Heliers Street, Abbotsford T *03 9417 5806* W *www.farm.org.au (Farmers Market second Saturday of each month)*

COMER, CAMERON – HOME ACCESSORIES DESIGNER/STYLIST
Comer & King M *0408 551 776* E *mail@comerandking.com* W *www.comerandking.com*

COUNTER AT CRAFT VICTORIA,
31 Flinders Lane, Melbourne T *03 9650 7775* W *www.craftvic.asn.au*

COWAN, EMMA – CARD DESIGNER/ARTIST
Threadcards T *03 9416 4131* M *0407 847 323* E *emmaloucowan@fastmail.fm* W *www.threadcards.com Stockists include Luft (see listing); Brunswick Street Bookstore, 305 Brunswick Street, Fitzroy* T *03 9416 1030; and Readings, 112 Acland Street, St Kilda* T *03 9525 3852*

CRAFT VICTORIA,
31 Flinders Lane, Melbourne T *03 9650 7775* W *www.craftvic.asn.au*

THE DANCING QUEEN,
327 Lennox Street, Richmond T *03 9425 9733* W *www.thedancingqueen.com.au*

DAVID ATKINS DESIGNS – GOLD & SILVERSMITH
T 03 9878 7130 W *www.davidatkins.com.au*

DAVIDSON, MARCOS – JEWELLER
room 7, level 7, Carlow House, 289 Flinders Lane,
Melbourne T *03 9654 1271* E *augusto@aapt.net.au*

DAVIS MUSIC CENTRE,
27 Byron Street, Footscray T *03 9689 2608*

DE KUIJER, KYLE, AND FLEMMING,
STEPHANIE – HOMEWARES DESIGNERS
Holly Daze E *info@hollydaze.com.au*
W *www.hollydaze.com.au Stockists include*
Craft Victoria (see listing); Heide Museum of Modern
Art (see listing); and Wilkins and Kent (see listing)

DELANY, MOYA –
FASHION ACCESSORIES DESIGNER
T *03 9427 9908* E *moya_delany@yahoo.com Stockists*
include Christine (see listing) and Le Louvre,
74 Collins Street, Melbourne T *03 9650 1300*

DE MILLE DECORATIVE & FINE ARTS,
7 Crossley Street, Melbourne T *03 9663 9666*

DEVILLE, JULIA – JEWELLER/TAXIDERMIST
Disce Mori M *0414 617 350* E *julia@discemori.com*
W *www.discemori.com Stockists include Cose Ipanema,*
113 Collins Street, Melbourne T *03 9650 3457; FAT,*
209 Brunswick Street, Fitzroy T *03 9486 0391 and*
272 Chapel Street, Prahran T *03 9510 2311*
W *www.fat4.com; and Nom*d Inc, 203 Gertrude Street,*
Fitzroy T *03 9416 3500*

DI BARTOLO, MARIANNA – BISCUIT AND
SWEET MAKER
Dolcetti M *0425 739 817* E *dolcetti@optusnet.com.au*
Stockists include Mr Tulk Cafe, 328 Swanston Street,
Melbourne T *03 8660 5700; Teaspoon,*
543a High Street, Prahran T *03 9521 4807; and*
Wall Two 80, 280 Carlisle Street, Balaclava
T *03 9593 8280*

DISCE MORI,
see **DEVILLE, JULIA**

DICKINS, SARA
see **WATERSON, ALANA**

DOMAIN FLOWERS,
183 Domain Road, South Yarra T *03 9820 1588*

DORMEUIL,
level 10, 22 William Street, Melbourne T *03 9629 9900*

DOUGLAS & HOPE
See **HOPE, CATHY**

DWYER, BRENDAN – SHOEMAKER
Brendan Dwyer Custom Made M *0411 676 572*
E *goblin@labyrinth.net.au (by commission)*

EAST AND WEST ART GALLERY,
665 High Street, Kew East T *03 9859 6277*

E.G.ETAL,
185 Little Collins Street, Melbourne T *03 9663 4334*
and 167 Flinders Lane, Melbourne T *03 9639 5111*
W *www.egetal.com.au*

ELLIOT SALON,
50 Davis Avenue, South Yarra T *03 9866 1811*

THE EMBROIDERERS GUILD OF VICTORIA,
170 Wattletree Road, Malvern T *03 9509 2222*

EMMERICHS, BERN – CERAMICIST
13 Hornby Street, Windsor T *03 9530 2507*
M *0400 162 537* E *gbemmerichs@primusonline.com.au*
Stockist details melbournestyle, 155 Clarendon Street,
South Melbourne T *03 9696 8445*

EMPIRE VINTAGE,
63 Cardigan Place, Albert Park T *03 9682 6677*
W *www.empirevintage.com.au*

EMPORIUM BOTANICA,
1018 High Street, Armadale T *03 9509 9111*

EST AUSTRALIA,
134 Auburn Road, Hawthorn East T *03 9819 0726*
M *0418 336 275 Soaps available at Red Hill Market,*
Arthur's Seat Road, Red Hill (first Saturday of each
month); see also **IMLACH, CAROLYN**

EUROTRASH,
228 Chapel Street, Prahran T *03 9510 4080*

EXHIBIT INTERIORS,
shop 67-69 Collins Place, Exhibition Street, Melbourne
T *03 9663 6333*

FEDERATION SQUARE,
corner Swanston and Flinders Streets, Melbourne
T *03 9655 1900* W *www.fedsquare.com*

FETHERS, GEORGE & CO. TRADING,
216 Rouse Street, Port Melbourne T *03 9646 5266*
W *www.gfethers.com.au*

FISHER, LACHLAN – CRICKET BAT MAKER
Fisher Hand-Crafted Cricket Bats,
295a Geelong Road, Kingsville T *03 9687 7848*
E *lachlan@fisherbats.com.au* W *www.fisherbats.com.au*

FLEMING, JULIE – MILLINER
Julie Fleming Melbourne, 456 Malvern Road,
Hawksburn T *03 9525 2456* M *0413 886 720*
E *juliefleming@bigpond.net.au*
W *www.juliefleming.com.au*

FLEMMING, STEPHANIE
see **DE KUIJER, KYLE**

GABRIEL, NIKKI –
KNITWEAR AND TEXTILE DESIGNER
E *nikkigab@bigpond.net.au* W *www.nikkigabriel.com*
Stockists include Husk (see listing); Cactus Jam,
12 Albert Coates Lane, Melbourne T *03 9654 0472;*
and RPM, 350 Lygon Street, Carlton T *03 9347 4245*

GALLERY FUNAKI,
4 Crossley Street, Melbourne T *03 9662 9446*
W *www.galleryfunaki.com.au*

GANIM, FRED – TILE PAINTER
M *0415 061 071* E *fredganim@hotmail.com*

GEORGIE LOVE (SALLY MORRIGAN)
M *0438 047 068* W *www.georgielove.com*
E *sally@georgielove.com*

GERNER, ANTON – FURNITURE MAKER
Anton Gerner Furniture, 24 Victoria Road,
Hawthorn East (by appointment only and by direct
commission) T *03 9813 2422*
E *info@antongerner.com.au* W *www.antongerner.com.au*

GERTRUDE CONTEMPORARY ART SPACES,
200 Gertrude Street, Fitzroy T *03 9419 3406*
W *www.gertrude.org.au*

GOLDEN, WENDY – BASKET MAKER
T *03 9808 2805* E *wendy@wendygolden.com*
W *www.wendygolden.com Stockists include Artisan*
Books (see listing); Craft Victoria (see listing); and
Moss Melbourne, 576 Malvern Road, Hawksburn
T *03 9525 0690; and 149 Fitzroy Street, St Kilda*
T *03 9525 5014*

GOLOTTA, FIORINA – JEWELLER
Fiorina Jewellery T *03 9826 2088*
E *fiorina@bigpond.net.au*

GOUGH, CAMILLA – JEWELLER
M *0405 537 511* E *camilla@camillagough.com*
W *www.camillagough.com Stockists e.g.etal (see listing)*

GRANT, ALEX W VIOLINS,
26 Smith Street, Collingwood
T *03 9417 4930* W *www.grantviolins.com.au*

GRAINGER MUSEUM,
University of Melbourne, Royal Parade, Parkville
T *03 8344 5270*
W *www.lib.unimelb.edu.au/collections/grainger/*

THE GREVILLE STREET BOOKSTORE,
145 Greville Street, Prahran T *03 9510 3531*

GWENDOLYNNE,
see **BURKIN, GWENDOLYNNE**

HABY, GRACIA AND JENNISON, LOUISE –
JOURNAL MAKERS/ARTISTS
hammer & daisy M *0412 144 472*
E *gracialouise@optusnet.com.au* W *www.gracialouise.*
com or www.gracialouise.com/catalog/ Stockists include
Craft Victoria (see listing); the Greville Street Bookstore
(see listing); and Wilkins and Kent (see listing)

HAMER HALL (MELBOURNE CONCERT HALL),
the Arts Centre, 100 St Kilda Road, Melbourne
T *03 9281 8000* W *www.theartscentre.net.au*

THE HANDWEAVERS AND SPINNERS
GUILD OF VICTORIA,
12-20 Shakespeare Street, Carlton North
T *03 9347 3008* W *http://home.vicnet.net.au/~handspin/*

HARING (KEITH) MURAL,
Northern Melbourne Institute of TAFE (Collingwood
campus), Johnston Street, Collingwood

R J HARVEY & CO,
level 3, 37 Swanston Street, Melbourne T *03 9654 7047*

HASLAM, VICTORIA – KNITWEAR DESIGNER
Pygmalion Handknits T *03 9899 8014*
E *yellavixen@hotmail.com Stockists include Hawthorn*
Craft Market (first Sunday of month, 10am-3pm
March-December) Hawthorn Town Hall,
358 Burwood Road, Hawthorn and Craft Victoria
(see listing)

HATTON, GREG – FURNITURE MAKER
M *0411 624 712* E *groggy_99@yahoo.com Stockists*
Juliet Horsley Homeware Design, 88 Park Road,
Middle Park T *03 9534 0633 and Julian Ronchi*
Garden Design and Nursery, 863 High Street,
Armadale T *03 9509 9882*

HEIDE MUSEUM OF MODERN ART,
7 Templestowe Road, Bulleen T *03 9850 1500*
W *www.heide.com.au*

HEMDEN MASTER SHIRTMAKERS & TAILORS,
see **NOTERMANS, EUGENE**

HERMON & HERMON,
556 Swan Street, Richmond T *03 9427 0599*
W *www.hermonhermon.com.au*

**HERRING ISLAND ENVIRONMENTAL
SCULPTURE PARK,**
*access by punt from Como Landing, Alexander Avenue,
opposite Como Park, South Yarra*

HIGHETT METAL,
283-295 Boundary Road, Braeside T *03 9587 7080*
W *www.highettmetal.com.au*

HOLLY DAZE,
see **DE KUIJER, KYLE**

HONEYWEATHER & SPEIGHT,
see **CATTELL, JAMES**

HOPE, CATHY – QUILTER
Douglas & Hope, 181 Brunswick Street, Fitzroy
T *03 9417 0662 and shop 14, the Block Arcade,
Elizabeth Street, Melbourne* T *03 9650 0585*

HOUND DOG'S BOP SHOP,
313 Victoria Street, West Melbourne T *03 9329 5362*

HUDSON CLOTHES,
229 Carlisle Street, Balaclava T *03 9525 8066*

HUSK,
123 Dundas Place, Albert Park T *03 9690 6994;
176 Collins Street, Melbourne* T *03 9663 0655; and
557 Malvern Road, Toorak* T *03 9827 2700*

IAN POTTER CENTRE
(see National Gallery of Victoria Australia)

IMLACH, CAROLYN – SOAP MAKER
Est Australia, 134 Auburn Road, Hawthorn East
T *03 9819 0726* M *0418 336 275*

INDUSTRIA,
202 Gertrude Street, Fitzroy T *03 9417 1117*
E *maxwatts@optusnet.com.au*

INNER CITY GARDEN SUPPLIES,
6 Kirkdale Street, Brunswick East T *03 9380 6772*

IRWIN AND McLAREN BOOKBINDERS
64 Cubitt Street, Richmond T *03 9428 5829*
E *info@irwinandmclaren.com.au*
W *www.irwinandmclaren.com.au*

JACKSON, BRUCE – GLASS GILDING ARTIST
Gold Reverre, 38 Yarra Street, Warrandyte
T *03 9844 2200* M *0412 321 252*
E *afl@goldreverre.com* W *www.goldreverre.com*

JACKSON, MELISSA – MILLINER
Shop – 195 Gertrude Street, Fitzroy T *03 9415 8836;
studio – 1 Harwood Place, Melbourne* T *03 9662 3272*
E *melissafashion@hotmail.com Stockists include
Christine (see listing); Assin (see listing) and Myer,
Bourke Street Mall, 295 Lonsdale Street, Melbourne*
T *03 9661 1111*

JANE'S ADDICTION CAKES,
see **WIFFEN, JANE**

JENNISON, LOUISE,
see **HABY, GRACIA**

JENNY PIHAN FINE ART,
*Kananook Creek Boathouse Gallery,
368 Nepean Highway, Frankston* T *03 9770 5354*
W *www.jennypihanfineart.com.au*

JOB WAREHOUSE FABRIC SALES,
56 Bourke Street, Melbourne T *03 9662 1603*

JUST TOOLS,
180 Clarendon Street, South Melbourne
T *03 9696 5722* W *www.justtools.com.au*

KANELA SPANISH FLAMENCO BAR,
56 Johnston Street, Fitzroy T *03 9419 0424*

**KAZARI COLLECTOR
(CONTEMPORARY ART AND ANTIQUES),**
450 Malvern Road, Prahran T *03 9529 5639*
W *www.kazari.com.au*

KAZARI WAREHOUSE AND ZIGUZAGU,
7-11 Hill Street, Richmond T *03 9427 1148*
W *www.kazari.com.au*

KENT, STEPHEN
see **WILKINS, JEREMY**

KEYHOLE ENGRAVING CO,
*shop 16a, Port Phillip Arcade, 232 Flinders Street,
Melbourne* T *03 9650 1791*

KOKO BLACK,
shop 4, Royal Arcade, 335 Bourke Street, Melbourne
T *03 9639 8911; 167 Lygon Street, Carlton*
T *03 9349 2775, and shop B118, Chadstone Shopping
Centre, 1341 Dandenong Road, Chadstone*
T *03 9530 9060* W *www.kokoblack.com*

KOZMINSKY JEWELLERY AND ART,
421 Bourke Street, Melbourne T *03 9670 1277*
W *www.kozminsky.com.au*

LANCASTER, PETER – LITHOGRAPHER
Lancaster Press T *03 9314 3036*
E *peterlancaster@ozemail.com.au*
W *www.lancasterpress.com.au*

LEFFLER, H, & SON LEATHER MERCHANTS,
50-66 York Street, South Melbourne T *03 9690 3577*
W *www.leffler.com.au*

LEWIS, ADRIAN – JEWELLER
29a Toorak Road, South Yarra T *03 9866 1533*

LIBBY EDWARDS GALLERIES,
1046 High Street, Armadale T *03 9509 8292*
W *www.libbyedwardsgalleries.com*

LINDA BLACK RECYCLED FASHION,
151 Chapel Street, Windsor T *03 9510 3948*

THE LITTLE BOOKROOM,
771 Nicholson Street, Carlton North T *03 9387 9837*

LLOYD, SIMON – PRODUCT DESIGNER
*Sisu, rear Kinross House, Toorak Uniting Church,
603 Toorak Road, Toorak (by appointment only)*
T *9578 1258* E *simonlloyd@sisu.com.au*
W *www.sisu.com.au*

LORGEN INTERNATIONAL DELI,
236 Carlisle Street, Balaclava T *03 9534 6121*

**LORENZETTO, ANNA –
LEATHER HOMEWARES DESIGNER**
Distributed by Taylor & Taylor Design T *03 9415 6586*
W *www.taylorandtaylordesign.com Stockist
Space Furniture, 629 Church Street, Richmond*
T *03 9426 3000* W *www.spacefurniture.com*

LUFT,
212 St Georges Road, Fitzroy North T *03 9489 0891*
W *www.luft.com.au*

LUSH,
116 Greville Street, Prahran T *03 9525 0166; and
250 Brunswick Street, Fitzroy* T *03 9415 1477*

**LUTZ, CARL – FURNITURE RESTORER AND
WOOD CARVER**
T *03 9751 1235*

McCLELLAND GALLERY AND SCULPTURE PARK,
390 McClelland Drive, Langwarrin T *03 9789 1671*
W *www.mcclellandgallery.com*

McLISKY, PETER – STONE CARVER
Peter McLisky Sculpture M *0411 619 925*
E *petermclisky@unite.com.au*
W *www.petermclisky.com.au*

MADE IN JAPAN,
260 Collins Street, Melbourne (and other locations)
T *03 9650 7303* W *www.mij.com.au*

MAIMONE, CHARLES – TAILOR
1 Crossley Street, Melbourne T *03 9662 1636*

MANCE, GEOFFREY – LIGHTING DESIGNER
Mance Design, 1 Campbell Street, Collingwood
T *03 9495 6425* W *www.mance.com.au*

MANCHESTER UNITY BUILDING,
corner Swanston and Collins Streets, Melbourne

MARAIS,
*level 1, Royal Arcade, 314 Little Collins Street,
Melbourne* T *03 9639 0314* W *www.marais.com.au*

MARINATO, MARK – MIRROR MAKER
Marinarto, head office, 18 Park Street, South Yarra
M *0412 007 632* E *markmarinato@marinarto.com*
W *www.marinarto.com Stockists include Coco
Republic, 500 Church Street, Richmond*
T *03 9421 2212; Kazari collector (see listing); and
Hermon & Hermon (see listing)*

MATTHYSEN, WILLIAM – CLOCK MAKER
48 Webb Street, Warrandyte T *03 9844 1250*
E *matthysen@bigpond.com*

MEAT MARKET CRAFT CENTRE,
42 Courtney Street, North Melbourne T *03 9322 3719*

MELBOURNE CRICKET GROUND,
Brunton Avenue, Richmond T *9657 8867*
W *www.mcg.org.au*

MELBOURNE OBSERVATION DECK,
*Rialto Towers, 525 Collins Street (corner King Street),
Melbourne* T *03 9629 8222*
W *www.melbournedeck.com.au*

E C MENZIES ELECTRICAL,
19 Ewing Street, Brunswick T *03 9387 5544*
W *www.ecmenzies.com.au*

THE MERCHANT OF FAIRNESS,
300 Whitehorse Road, Balwyn T *03 9836 7539 and
store 138, South Melbourne Market, York Street,
South Melbourne* T *03 9696 6545*
W *http://home.iprimus.com.au/cammicro/mof/*

METROPOLIS BOOKSHOP,
level 3, Curtin House, 252 Swanston Street, Melbourne
T *03 9663 2015*

**MIKEDIS, ANITA –
BOTANICAL HOMEWARES DESIGNER**
Evexia botanical gifts and home accessories
T *03 9443 8399* E *evexia@vtown.com.au*
W *www.evexia.com.au Stockists include Luft (see
listing); Roost Homewares (see listing) and Manque
Design, 70 High Street, Westgarth* T *03 9486 6701*

MISSING LINK RECORDS,
basement 405 Bourke Street, Melbourne
T *03 9670 8208* W *www.missinglink.net.au*

MURFETT, VICKI – SHELL ARTIST
E *vj_murfett@hotmail.com Stockist Christine
(see listing)*

**MURRAY, ADRIENNE – QUILT MAKER AND
PATCHWORK TEACHER**
*Patchwork on Central Park, 148 Burke Road,
Malvern East* T *03 9885 4480*

MUSEUM VICTORIA,
Nicholson Street, Carlton T *03 8341 7777*
W *museum.vic.gov.au*

MY DOG CAFE,
Station Pier, Port Melbourne T *9821 0669*
W *www.mydog.com.au*

**NATIONAL GALLERY OF VICTORIA AUSTRALIA
(THE IAN POTTER CENTRE),**
*Federation Square, corner Russell and Flinders Streets,
Melbourne* T *03 8620 2222.*
W *www.ngv.vic.gov.au/ngvaustralia/*

**NATIONAL GALLERY OF VICTORIA
INTERNATIONAL,**
180 St Kilda Road, Melbourne T *03 8620 2222*
W *www.ngv.vic.gov.au/ngvinternational/*

NATIVE AUSTRALIAN TIMBER ART,
shop 5, 1 Exhibition Street, Melbourne T *03 9662 3590*
M *0424 907 249* W *timberart.com.au*

NGV SHOP
*(see National Gallery of Victoria Australia and
National Gallery of Victoria International)*

NIAGARA GALLERIES,
245 Punt Road, Richmond T *03 9429 3666*
W *www.niagara-galleries.com.au*

NICHOLAS DATTNER AND COMPANY,
32 Gipps Street, Collingwood T *03 9417 5377*
W *www.nicholasdattner.com*

**NOTERMANS, EUGENE –
SHIRTMAKER/TAILOR**
*Hemden Master Shirtmakers and Tailors,
1024-1026 High Street, Armadale* T *03 9509 0933*
E *hemden@hemden.com.au* W *www.hemden.com.au*

NSW LEATHER CO,
107-109 Sackville Street, Collingwood T *03 9417 3466*
W *www.nswleather.com.au*

NYLON, RICHARD – MILLINER
71 Kerr Street, Fitzroy (by appointment only)
M *0400 967 251 Stockist Gwendolynne, 71 Kerr Street,
Fitzroy* T *03 9415 7687*

ODORCIC, MARY – JEWELLER
M *0411 299 636* E *maryodo@hotmail.com Stockists
include Alice Euphemia (see listing); Detail,
50 Glenferrie Road, Malvern and 80 Church Street,
Brighton; e.g.etal (see listing); and Pomme, 2a Watson
Road, Mount Martha*

THE OLD VILLAGE LOLLIE SHOP,
51 Anderson Street, Yarraville T *03 9687 3888*

OKE, NEIL – SURFBOARD MAKER
*Oke Surfboards, factory 1, 7 Canterbury Road,
Braeside* T *03 9587 3553*

O'KEEFE, BRENDAN – EYEWEAR DESIGNER
Brendan O'Keefe Eyewear W *www.brendanokeefe.com.au*

OTTOMAN CLASSICS,
155 Sydney Road, Brunswick T *03 9381 2235*
W *www.ottomanclassics.com*

OUTRÉ GALLERY,
249 Elizabeth Street, Melbourne T *03 9642 5455*
W *www.outregallery.com*

**PASCAL, MARC –
LIGHTING AND CERAMICS DESIGNER**
73 Newman Street, Thornbury (by appointment only)
T *03 9480 3617* E *marc@marcpascal.com*
W *www.marcpascal.com*

PELLEGRINI'S ESPRESSO BAR,
66 Bourke Street, Melbourne T *03 9662 1885*

PETROFF, LEON – VIOLIN MAKER
T *03 9557 5111* E *violins@leonpetroff.com.au*
W *www.leonpetroff.com.au*

PLUMRIDGE, CHRIS – CERAMICIST
Claystone Pottery T *03 9553 3330*
E *cplum@vicnet.net.au*
W *www.home.vicnet.net.au/~cplum Stockists Craft Victoria (see listing) and Wilkins and Kent (see listing)*

POLLARD, TIFFANY (JEWELLER),
level 5, Nicholas Building, 37 Swanston Street, Melbourne T *03 9663 3064* M *0410 470 755*

POMPEI, JACK, BOAT BUILDER
Pompei's of Mordialloc, 561 Main Street, Mordialloc T *03 9580 2033*

POPPIES FOR GRACE,
see **WATERSON, ALANA**

PRESTON, JOHANNA, AND ZLY, PETR – SHOEMAKERS
Preston Zly Design, rear 219 Smith Street, Fitzroy T *03 9417 2176* E *info@prestonzlydesign.com* W *www.prestonzlydesign.com*

PUGLISI, BENEDICT G. – STRINGED INSTRUMENT MAKER
Atelier Puglisi, 40 Church Street, Hawthorn T *03 9853 9525* E *bass@benedictgpuglisi.com* W *www.atelierpuglisi.com*

QUEEN VICTORIA MARKET,
(Tuesdays and Thursdays 6am-2pm, Fridays 6am-6pm and Sundays 9am-4pm) corner Elizabeth and Victoria Streets, Melbourne T *03 9320 5822* W *www.qvm.com.au*

RED STITCH ACTORS THEATRE,
rear 2 Chapel Street, St Kilda T *03 9533 8082*

RENAISSANCE BOOKBINDING,
493 Brunswick Street, Fitzroy North T *03 9481 8402*

RETRO-ACTIVE FURNITURE,
307 High Street, Northcote T *03 9489 4566* M *0411 096 367*

REVERSE ART TRUCK,
17 Greenwood Avenue, Ringwood T *03 9879 1264*

RICHARDS, BARBARA – LAMPSHADE MAKER
Sector 6, 140 St Kilda Road, St Kilda (by appointment) T *03 9525 5523 Stockists include Roost Homewares (see listing) and In the Bag, 521 High Street, Prahran* T *03 9525 0120*

RIPE – AUSTRALIAN PRODUCE,
376 Mount Dandenong Tourist Road, Sassafras T *03 9755 2100*

ROOST HOMEWARES,
256 Glenferrie Road, Malvern T *03 9509 7166*

ROSE STREET ARTISTS' MARKET
(Saturdays 11am-5pm), 60 Rose Street, Fitzroy T *03 9419 5529* M *0410 138 686* W *www.rosestmarket.com.au*

ROYAL BOTANIC GARDENS MELBOURNE,
Birdwood Avenue, South Yarra T *03 9252 2300* W *www.rbg.vic.gov.au*

RUBBLE & RICHES MARKET (LAVERTON MARKET),
(Saturday and Sunday 7am-4pm) 8 Leakes Road, Laverton T *03 9369 6426* M *0418 314 008* W *www.market.com.au*

RUSSELL, STEWART – TEXTILE PRINTER/ARTIST
Spacecraft, level 1, GPO Melbourne, corner Bourke and Elizabeth Streets, Melbourne T *03 9662 2012; studio* T *03 9329 4129* E *info@spacecraftaustralia.com* W *www.spacecraftaustralia.com*

ST ANDREWS MARKET,
(Saturdays 8am-2pm) corner Kangaroo Ground and St Andrews Roads, St Andrews T *03 9756 7515*

ST KILDA BOWLING CLUB,
66 Fitzroy Street, St Kilda T *03 9537 0370*

ST KILDA ESPLANADE ARTS AND CRAFT MARKET
(Sundays 10am-5pm), Upper Esplanade, between Cavell and Fitzroy Streets, St Kilda T *03 9534 0066* W *www.esplanademarket.com*

ST KILDA SALVATION ARMY FAMILY STORE,
90 Inkerman Street, St Kilda T *03 9534 3514*

ST LUKE ARTIST COLOURMEN,
32 Smith Street, Collingwood T *03 9486 9992* W *www.langridgecolours.com*

ST PATRICK'S CATHEDRAL,
corner Gisborne Street and Cathedral Place, East Melbourne T *9662 2233* W *www.melbourne.catholic.org.au/cathedral*

SARTI TAILORS (CELIA COATE AND PEPPINO TAVELLA),
shop 6, 144 Little Collins Street, Melbourne T *03 9639 7811* E *celia@sarti.com.au* W *www.sarti.com.au*

SAUNDERS, JOANNE – RECORDER MAKER
M *0409 143 942* E *jgsrecs@bigpond.net.au*

SCHOOF, JOANNE – CANDLE MAKER
A Little Light M *0402 547 362*
E *joanne@alittlelight.com.au* W *www.alittlelight.com.au*
*Stockists include Hermon & Hermon (see listing) and
Husk (see listing)*

SHAG,
377 Brunswick Street North, Fitzroy T *03 9417 3348;
shop 20, Centre Way Arcade, Collins Street,
Melbourne* T *03 9663 8166 and 130 Chapel Street,
Windsor* T *03 9510 8817*

SHEIL, MARK – METAL ARTISAN
Sheil Abbey and Gallery, 21 Carpenter Street, Brighton
T *03 9592 8192 and 53 Toorak Road, South Yarra*
T *03 9866 6866* W *www.sheilabbey.com.au*

SHIBATA, MASAKO – TEXTILE ARTIST
Shima Blue, 19 Bendigo Street, North Melbourne
T *03 9326 3184* E *info@shimablue.com*
W *www.shimablue.com Stockists include Made in
Japan, Australia on Collins, 260 Collins Street,
Melbourne* T *03 9650 7303; Nest Homewares,
289-291 Coventry Street, South Melbourne*
T *03 9699 8277; and Luft (see listing)*

SMITH, C.H, MARINE,
16 Langridge Street, Collingwood T *03 9417 1077*
W *www.chsmith.com.au*

SMITTEN KITTEN,
shop 6, Degraves Street, Melbourne T *03 9654 2073*
W *www.smittenkitten.com.au*

SOMEDAY GALLERY,
*level 3b, Curtin House, 252 Swanston Street,
Melbourne* T *03 9654 6458*

SONSA FOODS,
152 Smith Street, Collingwood T *03 9417 1706*

SPACECRAFT
see **RUSSELL, STEWART**

SPACE FURNITURE,
629 Church Street, Richmond T *03 9426 3000*
W *www.spacefurniture.com*

SPAN GALLERIES,
45 Flinders Lane, Melbourne T *03 9650 0589*
W *www.spangalleries.com.au*

SPIRA, JACK – GUITAR MAKER
Jack Spira Guitars by commission T *03 5968 1625*
E *jack@jackspiraguitars.com*
W *www.jackspiraguitars.com*

STEP BACK ANTIQUES,
103 Burwood Road, Hawthorn T *03 9815 0635*
M *0418 334 475*

STEWART, ADAM – CONTEMPORARY FURNITURE MAKER
Nico Design, 42 Courtney Street, North Melbourne
T *03 9326 8553* M *0407 869 921*
E *adamstewart@iprimus.com.au*

STICKY,
*shop 10, Campbell Arcade (off Degraves Street),
Melbourne* T *03 9654 8559* W *www.platform.org.au*

STOKES, PHILIP – GLASS ARTIST
*Philip Stokes Studio Glass, Abbotsford Convent
Mercator Laundry, 1 St Heliers Street, Abbotsford*
T *03 9415 7959* M *0421 733 257*
E *info@philipstokesstudioglass.com.au*
W *www.philipstokesstudioglass.com.au Stockists include
Charles Smith Gallery, 65 Smith Street, Fitzroy*
T *03 9419 0880; Glass Plus Gallery, 284 Park Street,
South Melbourne* T *03 9696 4776; and Veronica
George Gallery (see listing)*

SUGA,
shop 20 Royal Arcade, 335 Bourke Street, Melbourne
T *03 9663 5654 and other locations* W *www.suga.com.au*

SYBER'S BOOKS,
668 Glenhuntly Road, Caulfield South T *03 9523
6686, and 38 Chapel Street, Windsor* T *03 9530 2222*

THOMSON, MATT – BAG MAKER
M *0411 040 214* E *mattt@mattt.com.au*
W *www.mattt.com.au Stockists include the Arts Centre
Sunday Market, St Kilda Road, Melbourne, and
Village Idiom, 34 Anderson Street, Yarraville*
T *03 9687 3445*

T L WOOD FASHION BOUTIQUE,
216 Chapel Street, Prahran T *03 9510 6700*

TOLARNO GALLERIES,
level 4, 289 Flinders Lane, Melbourne T *03 9654 6000*
W *www.tolarnogalleries.com*

TOTALLY GOURDGEOUS,
band, W *www.totallygourdgeous.com*

TRAEGER, LYNLEY – JEWELLER/ WALKING STICK MAKER
*Room 6, level 6, Nicholas Building,
37 Swanston Street, Melbourne* M *0413 097 807*
By appointment only and commission only

THE TRAVELLERS
sculpture by Nadim Karam, with City of Melbourne designers and ARUP engineers, Sandridge Bridge (spanning Yarra River from Southbank Boulevard to Queensbridge Street), Melbourne

TUCKER, JESSIE – LINGERIE DESIGNER
T *03 9419 1144* W *www.jessietucker.net*
E *info@jessietucker.net Stockists include Kitty K (see listing); Smitten Kitten (see listing); and Scally and Trombone, 331 Brunswick Street, Fitzroy*
T *03 9419 6038*

TUCKER, KATE – TEXTILE/HANDBAG MAKER
Katarzynkha Bags W *www.katarzynkha.com*
T *03 9419 1144 Stockist information Gorman, 253 Brunswick Street, Fitzroy* T *03 9419 5999*

T2,
340 Brunswick Street, Fitzroy T *03 9416 2216 and other locations* W *www.t2tea.com.au*

UHE, LAURA – DANCE TEACHER
T *03 9822 8130* M *0414 260 236*
E *amefryer@bigpond.com.au*

UNTIL NEVER GALLERY,
level 2, 3-5 Hosier Lane, Melbourne
E *info2@citylightsproject.com* W *www.citylightsproject.com*

VEG OUT COMMUNITY GARDENS ST KILDA,
corner Shakespeare Grove and Chaucer Street, St Kilda E *hello@vegout.asn.au* W *www.vegout.asn.au*

VERONICA GEORGE GALLERY,
1082 High Street, Armadale T *03 9500 9930*

VIDEO BUSTERS,
134 Smith Street, Collingwood T *03 9417 2269 and other locations*

VIXEN,
see **CHAPMAN, GEORGIA**

WATCHORN, IAN – STRINGED INSTRUMENT MAKER
T *03 9853 1401* E *Ian@IanWatchorn.com.au*
W *www.ianwatchorn.com.au*

WATERSON, ALANA, AND DICKINS, SARA – STATIONERY DESIGNERS
Poppies for Grace, M *0400 919 145 (Alana) and 0438 520 384 (Sara)* W *info@poppiesforgrace.com*
W *www.poppiesforgrace.com*

WHEELER, BECK – ARTIST/TEXTILE SCULPTOR
E *beck@beckwheeler.net* W *www.beckwheeler.net*
W *www.kissykissytoys.com Stockists include Craft Victoria (see listing) and Georgie Love (see listing)*

WHITE, ILKA – WEAVER AND TEXTILE DESIGNER
T *03 9654 8659* E *ilka@ilka.com.au*
W *www.ilka.com.au Stockists e.g.etal (see listing) and Craft Victoria (see listing)*

WIFFEN, JANE – CUPCAKE MAKER
Jane's Addiction Cakes M *0414 940 458 Available at Per Tutti, shop 2, 20 Chatham Street, Prahran*
T *03 9521 5553*

WILKINS, JEREMY, AND KENT, STEPHEN – FURNITURE MAKERS
Wilkins and Kent, 230 Brunswick Street, Fitzroy
T *03 9419 5251* E *info@wilkinsandkent.com*
W *www.wilkinsandkent.com*

WILLIAMS, MAUREEN – GLASS ARTIST
T *03 9525 4313* E *maureenwilliams@ozemail.com.au*
Stockists include Axia Modern Art, 1010 High Street, Armadale T *03 9500 1144; Potoroo, U10, upper level, Southgate* T *03 9690 9859 and Cellini Workshop, Queens Parade, Clifton Hill* T *03 9482 3490*

WONDOFLEX YARN CRAFT CENTRE,
1353 Malvern Road, Malvern T *03 9822 6231*
W *www.wondoflex.com.au*

WOOD, ANDREW – WOOD WORKER
T *03 9482 5589* E *a.wood@optusnet.com.au*
W *www.andrewwood.net Stockist Craft Victoria (see listing)*

WYNNE, CHRIS – GUITAR MAKER
Thomas Lloyd School of Guitar Making
T *03 9431 2490* M *0403 910 880*
W *www.thomaslloydguitars.com*

ZLY, PETR,
see **PRESTON JOHANNA**

ZOMP SHOEZ,
271 Little Collins Street, Melbourne T *03 9639 6728 and shop 9, 546 Chapel Street, South Yarra*
T *03 9827 1933*